James
Harrod

James Harrod

FOUNDER OF
HARRODSBURG, KENTUCKY

BOBBI DAWN RIGHTMYER

THE
History
PRESS

Published by The History Press
Charleston, SC
www.historypress.com

First published 2023

Manufactured in the United States

ISBN 9781467154475

Library of Congress Control Number: 2023932152

This book is dedicated to the citizens of Harrodsburg—past, present and future. I hope it stirs curiosity about the past of our historic town.

It is also dedicated to my family: Keith Rightmyer; Christopher and Dee Castillo-Rightmyer; Marie and Devon Huffman; and Amber, Jason, Logan and Abigail Wilham.

Contents

Acknowledgements 9
Timeline. James Harrod, Founder of Harrodsburg 11

1. Early Life 21
2. 1773: The Western Fever 30
3. 1774: First Permanent Settlement West of the
     Allegheny Mountains 43
4. 1775: The Transylvania Company 54
5. 1776: Creating Kentucky County 73
6. 1777: Year of the Bloody Sevens 87
7. 1778: James Harrod Takes a Wife 106
8. 1779–1780: The Hard Winter and Beyond 114
9. 1781–1782: Kentucky at a Crossroad 126
10. 1783–1784: The First Courts at Harrodstown 135
11. 1785–1786: The Civilization of Kentucky 139
12. 1787–1792: Onward to Statehood 145

Appendix. Incidental Information Regarding James Harrod 153
Notes 167
Bibliography 179
About the Author 187

Acknowledgements

A s a writer of narrative nonfiction history, I have relied on research libraries and newspapers archives, as well as county records and personal recollections from Harrodsburg natives, to collect the information for this book. A long journey begins with just one step, and the journey of this book staggered into a great number of fine folks who offered knowledge and expertise. I can't thank them all personally, but I will name as many as possible. My sincerest apologies to any I missed.

First and foremost, I want to thank my husband, Keith Rightmyer, for his support, encouragement and photography skills, without which this book would not have been possible.

Secondly, I want to thank the following institutions and their employees for their assistance and inspiration: Harrodsburg Historical Society, Kentucky Historical Society, Filson Historical Society, Boyle County Historical Society, Capital City Museum, James Harrod Trust, Mercer County Chamber of Commerce, Harrodsburg First, Harrodsburg/Mercer County Tourism Commission, Armstrong Archives, Joseph's Dream, Springfield Historical Society, Mercer County Public Library, Boyle County Public Library, Harvey Helm Memorial Library, Centre College Grace Doherty Library, Deal Library in the United Kingdom, Mercer County Deed Records, Shaker Village of Pleasant Hill, University of Louisville, University of Kentucky, Transylvania University, *Harrodsburg Herald*, *Kentucky Democrat*, *Advocate-Messenger*, *Lexington Herald-Leader*, *Courier-Journal*, *Draper Manuscripts*, *Argus of Western America* and the History Press publishing team.

I also want to thank several local citizens for their encouragement and resources: Jerry L. Sampson, Stuart Sanders, Helen Dedman, Jill Cutler, Kandie Adkinson, Amalie Preston, Kay Keightley Foster, Marian Bauer, Kelly Scott Reed, Susan Thompson Barrington, Mary Cecil Thompson, Lisa Botner Goodrich, JoEtta Y. Wickliffe, Marsha Noel, Sarah Woods Bottom, Elizabeth Blair Bottom, Nancy Hill, Anna Armstrong, Mel Stewart Hankla and Michael Wisner.

A special thank-you to Larry Neuzel for scanning and formatting the photographs for this book. Without his help, there would be no photographs for readers to view.

Lastly, I could not have completed this book without the efforts of History Press acquisitions editor Chad Rhoad; Chad kept me plugging away. Thank you.

DISCLAIMER: The term *Indian* for Native Americans was commonly used and accepted during the time of James Harrod and the pioneers. It is not our intention to offend any ethnic group by its use in the text, so with a few exceptions the author has replaced the word *Indian* with Native American. The word *Indian* is used when historically accurate in a direct quote.

Timeline

JAMES HARROD, FOUNDER OF HARRODSBURG

1734
John Harrod Sr. comes to America from England.

1736
The widower John Harrod marries Sarah Moore.

Circa 1742–46
James Harrod is born. The exact date and year are unknown.

1754
John Harrod Sr. dies at Great Cove.

1755
Sarah Harrod flees the Great Cove with her remaining family and settles
near Fort Littleton.
   July 9. John Harrod Jr. is injured while under Lieutenant Colonel
   George Washington's command.

1756
James and William Harrod work on the Forbes Road, a provincial militia
roadway.

1758

James serves under Brigadier General John Forbes in the Fort Duquesne campaigns during the French and Indian War.

1759

Sarah moves the family again, this time to the south fork of Tenmile Creek in the Monongahela area of Pennsylvania.

1760

June. Harrod volunteers as one of Captain Gavin Cochran's militia.

1763

James Harrod joins Henry Bouquet during the Fort Pitt campaign of Pontiac's Rebellion.

1767

Winter. George Washington conducts the first land surveys in Kentucky under the Proclamation of 1763.

Spring. James Harrod ventures into the area now known as Illinois to join his brother Samuel.

1772

Spring. James and William return to Kentucky and make friends with the Delaware Indians.

Summer. George Rogers Clark's first time to Kentucky.

October. Captain Thomas Bullitt (1730–1778) advertises an expedition into Kentucky for 1773 to make surveys for military land warrants.

1773

Spring. Harrod joins up with Captain Bullitt to survey land at the falls of the Ohio.

July 4. Harrod and Bullitt meet up with the McAfee brother at Big Bone Lick.

July 7. McAfee brothers reach the mouth of the Kentucky River at present-day Frankfort.

July 8. Harrod and Bullitt reach the falls of the Ohio at present-day Louisville.

Summer. McAfee brothers survey eight thousand acres around Salt River in Mercer County but construct no buildings.

September. Chief Cornstalk breaks the truce and directs a massacre of families on outlying stations.

September 25. Daniel Boone and family leave Yadkin Valley for Kentucky.

October 9. Daniel Boone's son Jamie is killed during an attack by bands of Delawares, Shawnees and Cherokees.

December. Lord Dunmore authorizes military warrants to be located anywhere in Virginia territory.

December 16. The Boston Tea Party takes place, with 342 chests of tea being dumped into the harbor.

1774

March. James Harrod and a company of thirty-one men start for Kentucky.

April 7. Harrod's party arrives at the Big Spring.

June 8. Captain William Russell sends Daniel Boone and Michael Stoner to warn Harrod of the increasing Indian hostilities.

June 16. Harrod's Town is founded when the pioneers draw up in-lots and out-lots and start construction.

Summer. The first corn crops are planted at Harrodsburg and Fountainbleu Spring.

June 27. Boone and Stoner start their journey to Kentucky.

June 28. Isaac Hite and his band of eleven men join Harrod at Harrod's Town. Hite founds Fountainbleu Spring.

July 16. Native American attack at Fountainbleu Spring takes place.

July 20. Boone and Stoner arrive at Harrod's Town, but Harrod and company had already left the area.

October 10. The Battle of Point Pleasant, or Lord Dunmore's War, takes place.

October 17. Lord Dunmore and members of the Shawnee, Mingo and Delaware Tribes sign the Treaty of Camp Charlotte.

1775

March 8. Harrod leads a group of forty men back to Harrod's Town to stay at the first permanent settlement in Kentucky.

March. Richard Henderson founds the Transylvania Company.

March. Henderson helps negotiate the Treaty of Sycamore Shoals with the Cherokees.

April 1. Daniel Boone arrives in Kentucky and lays out plans for Fort Boonesborough.

April 22. Construction on Fort Boonesborough begins.

May 7. James Harrod and Thomas Slaughter bring their land dispute to the Transylvania Company.

May 23. The Transylvania Assembly holds the first American legislative assembly west of the Appalachians.

June 14. Fort Boonesborough is completed.

September. William Pogue and family arrive at Boonesborough.

September. Hugh McGary and family arrive at Harrod's Town.

September. Construction on Fort Harrod begins.

October. St. Asaph's, also known as Logan's Station, is completed.

October. Harrod Wilson, the first European heritage child born in Kentucky, is born at Fort Harrod.

1776

February. William Pogue's family moves to Harrod's Town.

February. Fort Harrod is completed.

March. The Transylvania Company opens a land grant office at Fort Harrod.

April. Harrodsburg settlers send a petition to Virginia stating the great expense and many hardships in settling the country.

Spring. James Harrod and Benjamin Logan transport a quantity of lead from the Long Island of Holston, Tennessee.

Spring. In Kentucky, the population was estimated to be two hundred, with most people at Boonesborough, Harrod's Town and Logan's Station.

June. James Harrod loses faith in the Transylvania Company and becomes an outspoken opponent.

June 8–15. George Rogers Clark and Gabriel Jones are elected as delegates and are instructed to appeal to Virginia to overthrow Transylvania and incorporate the county under its own government.

June 12. Elizabeth Hays, eldest grandchild of Daniel Boone, is the first female of European heritage born in Kentucky.

June 20. A twenty-one-person Committee of Safety meets to prepare a petition for the Virginia Convention with their grievances.

July 14. Jemima Boone and Elizabeth and Frances Callaway are kidnapped by a band of Cherokees and Shawnees.

August. Clark and Jones leave with the petition for Virginia Convention.

August 23. Governor Patrick Henry sends five hundred pounds of gunpowder to Fort Pitt for Clark and Jones to pick up.

Autumn. Thomas Denton plants the first crop of wheat in Kentucky.

September 2. The first court in Kentucky County is held.

September. Clark stays for the fall legislature in Williamsburg.

November. Clark collects the gunpowder from Fort Pitt but is followed by Indians and has to bury the barrels.

December 24. Clark's group is ambushed by Shawnees trying to retrieve the gunpowder.

December 29. McClelland's Fort is attacked while pioneers tried to save the gunpowder.

December 31. Kentucky County is formed out of Fincastle County, Virginia.

1777

"Year of the Bloody Sevens."

January 3. The gunpowder is finally retrieved and delivered to Fort Harrod, where it is divided between the three main forts: Boonesborough, Logan's Station and Fort Harrod.

January 6. John McClelland dies of wounds received during the fort attack.

January 30. Clark escorts the widows, the orphans and remaining militiamen from McClelland's Station to Fort Harrod.

February. Because of Indian attacks, only three settlements remain in Kentucky: Fort Harrod, Logan's Station and Boonesborough.

February 27. Hugh McGary sends a memorial to Virginia's governor praying for aid and relief in their distressed situation.

March. Public dispatches arrive at Fort Harrod for the military and civil commissions for the officers of Kentucky County.

March 5. The militia of Kentucky County starts a regiment, with a company mustered from the three settlements.

March 6. The Shawnees, led by Chief Blackfish, attack Fort Harrod, but the fort does not fall.

March 7. The Shawnees burn cabins outside Fort Harrod.

March 28. The Shawnees again attack Fort Harrod, but the fort does not fall.

April 3. Michael Stoner arrives at Fort Harrod with news of attacks at Rye Cove on the Clinch River.

April 19. Even with continued attacks, Fort Harrod holds elections, and the wedding of James Berry to widow Christina Stagner Wilson (daughter of Barney Stagner) takes place.

May 1. The census at Harrod's Town records 201 residents.

June. Detroit lieutenant governor Henry Hamilton begins using Native Americans against the settlers in the West.

June 22. Barney Stagner is killed and scalped by the Native Americans near the Fort Harrod spring.

September. Colonel John Bowman arrives to lead the Kentucky militia.

September 2. The first court is held in Harrodsburg.

September 22. The corncrib skirmish at Cove Spring takes place.

Fall. Governor Patrick Henry approves George Rogers Clark's plan to push the British out of the Ohio Valley region.

1778

February. James Harrod marries Ann Coburn McDaniel at Logan's Station.

Fall. Harrod and his new wife finally move to Boiling Spring after renovations are completed.

Fall. The British are dealing with the repercussions of Colonel George Rogers Clark's victory at Kaskaskia.

October. Harrod and sixteen other men go to the falls of the Ohio to obtain salt for the winter.

1779

Winter. Harrod receives a permanent military commission as colonel.

Spring. A land office is opened in Harrodsburg.

November. A harsh winter begins and doesn't end until March 1780.

1780

Spring. James Harrod's brother Samuel is killed while returning to Harrodsburg from New Orleans.

June 22. British captain Henry Bird's militia, along with Native Americans, attacks Ruddle's Station.

July. Harrod sends a petition to the Continental Congress because of Kentucky's uncertain political status and dangers threatening the area.

August. Clark's campaign up the Little Miami River to intercept Captain Bird fails.

August 4. Captain Bird reaches Detroit with 155 prisoners of war.

Fall. Virginia does away with the county of Kentucky, setting up three new counties: Jefferson, Lincoln and Fayette.

1781

December 28. John Harrod Jr. dies.

1782

August 15–17. Battle of Bryan's Station takes place. Hugh McGary leads the Harrodsburg militia because Harrod is sick with lumbago.

August 19. Defeat at the Battle of Blue Licks, the last battle of the American Revolutionary War.

August 24. Captain Logan's militia arrives at Blue Lick in time to bury the dead.

September. Harrod and Clark lead another campaign to take Detroit, but bad weather ends this after only a few weeks.

1783

Spring. The first horse racing track, "Haggin's Race Path," begins operation in Harrodsburg.

Spring. Virginia restores Kentucky as a district and sets up a high court system that can finally handle capital cases.

Summer. Dan Broadhead opens a dry goods store in Louisville.

Summer. James Harrod establishes the first "man-made" beehive in Kentucky at Boiling Spring.

1784

November. Benjamin Logan calls the leading men of Kentucky to Danville to discuss the continued Indian problem.

December. The first constitutional convention of Kentucky is held in Danville and called by Colonel Benjamin Logan.

1785

September. Margaret Coburn Harrod is born to James and Ann Harrod, his only natural child.

October. The Virginia Assembly establishes the town "known by the name of Harrodstown as Harrodsburg, in the county of Lincoln."

Fall. Mercer County is formed from the land around Harrodsburg.

1786

Spring. James and Ann Harrod open the Latin School at Boiling Spring.

Spring. Hugh McGary is court-martialed because of his actions at Blue Licks.

Summer. The Methodist church holds its first quarterly conference at Boiling Spring.

1787

November. James McDaniel, stepson of James Harrod, is killed by Indians and burned at Boiling Spring.

December. The Latin School at Boiling Spring is closed.

1791

November 28. James Harrod prepares his will.

1792

Spring. James Harrod disappears while on a hunting trip and is never seen again.

June 1. During the tenth and final Danville convention in 1792, the constitution is drawn up. The Commonwealth of Kentucky is admitted into the union as the fifteenth state.

1793

August 13. James Harrod's seat on the Harrodsburg Board of Trustees is declared vacant.

December. James Harrod's will is probated.

1802

Ann Harrod marries a man named John Tadlock (circa 1802).

1804

December 15. John Tadlock sues for divorce from Ann.

1815
Andrew Gore buys Fort Harrod Spring, and it is renamed Gore's Spring.

1843
April. Ann Coburn Harrod dies and is buried at Boiling Spring.

1943
March 2. The SS *James Harrod* is launched.

1945
January 16. The SS *James Harrod* collides with the SS *Raymond B. Stevens* and burns in the North Sea.

Chapter 1

EARLY LIFE

James Harrod…matured into a slender man, an inch over six feet tall,
with black hair and a black beard.
—*Lowell H. Harrison and James C. Klotter,* A New History of Kentucky

Most people are familiar with the frontiersman Daniel Boone, but most do not recognize the name James Harrod. While Boone is famous for settling land in Kentucky during the mid- to late 1700s and founding Boonesborough, Harrod was the founder of Harrodsburg, the oldest permanent English settlement west of the Allegheny Mountains. Establishing Harrodsburg was a symbolic act declaring the Kentucky frontier open for settlement. These lands were no longer the exclusive hunting ground of the Native Americans, nor the unexplored wilderness of pioneers like Boone.[1]

While Boone is famous for opening up the Kentucky frontier and having numerous narratives published of his early experiences, Harrod, with little fanfare, was just as important in the early settlement process. Harrod was essential in early land surveys, the emerging court system and leading Kentucky on to statehood.

Very little is known about James Harrod's parents. His father, John, came from England about the year 1734, probably in search of a better life for himself, wife Caroline Downey and two sons, John Jr. and Thomas. This small family settled among the very first pioneers on the Shenandoah, in the valley of Virginia. It was a hard life, and Harrod's father soon

Portrait of Daniel Boone, 1820, oil on canvas. This was a gift from Mr. and Mrs. Arthur H. Almstedt. *Collection of the Speed Art Museum, Louisville, Kentucky.*

became a young widower when Native Americans came and burned their home and Caroline was killed. Thankfully, the two young boys were rescued by neighbors.[2]

John Harrod knew that he needed to find a new wife to care for his sons, so he moved to the Shenandoah Valley in Virginia and soon married Sarah Moore, daughter of James Moore and Frances Gay. The couple went on to have four sons (Samuel, William, James and Levi) and six daughters (Nellie,

Rachel, Mary, Sallie, Elizabeth and Jemima). After the birth of Samuel, the family moved to the Big Cove in present-day Bedford County, Pennsylvania.[3]

James Harrod was born in Bedford County, Pennsylvania, but his actual year of birth is disputed. Various sources list his birth year anywhere from 1742 to 1746, but the latter date is used by most historians. One source states that James was twelve years old when his father died in 1754; another states that he was not quite ten years old. Kentucky historian James Klotter has recorded that Harrod was only about fourteen years old when he fought in several battles of the French and Indian War before it ended in 1763. Klotter also noted that when Harrod volunteered as one of Captain Gavin Cochran's Recruits in June 1760, he listed his age at sixteen and his height at five feet, two and a half inches. This discrepancy from his adult height of more than six feet may show that he lied on his recruitment records.[4]

It is unclear when the Harrod family moved back to the Shenandoah Valley, but James was a baby. Unfortunately, the family didn't secure land titles before they staked their claim. Thomas Fairfax, Baron of Cameron, claimed to own Harrod's land, as evidence of a survey he had conducted in 1736 and 1737. Lord Fairfax's survey was registered in 1746, and this is when he demanded leases for all his lands. The Harrods refused to pay, so they crossed the Potomac River and made their way along Indian trails through west Maryland, north to Little Cove in the Kittatinny, a range of hills in eastern Pennsylvania and Virginia.[5]

Kittatinny was a Delaware word meaning "endless hills," and the Delaware Native Americans claimed the land west of the Kittatinny. This land was an area Great Britain had not claimed as a treaty purchase. Fearing Indian attacks, Harrod moved his family to the Conococoheague Valley, close to Pennsylvania frontier territory, finally settling north of the Great Cove Settlement, now current-day Fulton County.[6]

In 1754, near the outset of the French and Indian War, John Harrod Sr. died. Sarah's two stepsons, Thomas and John Jr., who were living in Baltimore with relatives, moved to be with her and the rest of the children. The widow was busy teaching all her children at home to read and write because she thought it was important. At this time, Samuel joined the Maryland militia, and James, already a skilled woodsman, was particularly adept at hunting, trapping and fishing. His skill with a rifle was particularly noteworthy.

In November 1755, fearing Indian uprisings, Sarah Harrod took the family and fled their home just before the celebrated Delaware warrior

JAMES HARROD.

The only known lithograph of James Harrod, the founder of Harrodsburg. *Kentucky Historical Society*.

King Shangas and his war party made a bloody descent on the Great Cove Settlement. It is reported that of the "ninety-three families which were settled in the Great Coves…forty-seven were either killed or taken and the rest deserted." The Native Americans killed some and captured others, while another portion was fortunate to escape with their lives when their cabins and possessions went up in flames.[7]

The Harrod family relocated to Fort Littleton at the foot of Cove Mountain near Bedford, Pennsylvania, and it was here that James and William began

Autograph of James Harrod.

THE FOUNDER OF HARRODSBURG.

Above: A facsimile of James Harrod's signature. *Harrodsburg Historical Society*.

Left: A black-and-white reproduction of an oil portrait painting of Thomas Fairfax, Sixth Lord Fairfax of Cameron. The original portrait is located at the Alexandria-Washington Lodge No. 22 A.F. & A.M. in Alexandria, Virginia.

their long military careers. They first served as rangers and guards and then as commissioned officers. James was the best marksman, and Will was strongest at hand-to-hand combat. They were continually competing with each other.

In 1758, James and William Harrod went on to serve under Brigadier General John Forbes in the Fort Duquesne campaigns during the French and Indian War. Fort Duquesne was destroyed by the French during the war and later replaced by Fort Pitt. The British had promised the soldiers land in Kentucky as payment for their services. Being raised on the frontiers with early training on border military service, Harrod had a love for hunting and wild-woods life, so the promise of land in Kentucky was a huge incentive to fight. Just like Daniel Boone, James Harrod was gaining a reputation as a great backwoodsman and frontiersman.[8]

Sarah eventually moved back to Conococoheague. John Jr. and Samuel joined Major General Edward Braddock to fight in the west. The British had sent General Braddock to fight against the French, and an ambitious Virginian named George Washington volunteered as Braddock's aide. John Jr. volunteered for expeditions under Lieutenant Colonel George Washington to assert Virginia's domination over the Forks of Ohio.[9]

This was a disastrous mission and John was injured. During this time, James and William joined James Burd as road builders to help survey and clear the way for the provincial militia roadway named Forbes Road. They worked on building the supply road to connect eastern Pennsylvania with the advancing British forces near the three forks of the Youghiogheny River.

The Harrod family moved again to the south fork of Tenmile Creek in the Monongahela area of Washington County, Pennsylvania. There was an abundance of trees: black walnut, chestnut, oak, sugar maples and hickory. Widow Sarah was happy and content, living the good life her sons were fighting for.[10]

In 1763, Harrod joined with Henry Bouquet during the Fort Pitt campaign of Pontiac's Rebellion, named for the leader of the Odawa, or Indigenous Americans of the North, Central and South America. This rebellion started in May 1763 because Delaware and Shawnee Indians were offended by the policies of British general Jeffrey Amherst. The legacy of Amherst is controversial because of his strong desire to exterminate the Native Americans. He advocated the use of biological warfare by gifting the indigenous people with blankets infected with smallpox: "You will do well to try to inoculate the Indians by means of blankets, as well as to try every other method, which can serve to extirpate this execrable race."[11]

A photo of Harrod's Station on Tenmile Creek in the Monongahela area of Washington County, Pennsylvania, circa 1770. *Colonel George Chinn Collection.*

In 1767, George Washington conducted the first land surveys in Kentucky under the Proclamation of 1763, with Samuel Harrod and Michael Stoner leading the campaign. During the spring of 1767, James Harrod ventured into the area now known as Illinois to join his brother Samuel. Samuel brought James to the Bluegrass Region of Kentucky in search of furs. They explored the headwaters of the Pigeon River, the current-day Salt River, in what is now Mercer County. The Salt River of north-central Kentucky is the commonwealth's fifth-largest watershed and was once a primary supplier of salt for the region. The brothers returned to their homes in the Pennsylvania border country enthusiastic about the possibility of claiming land in the new territory, which was then part of Virginia.[12]

In 1772, James accompanied his brother William to Tenmile Creek to visit his mother. By now Harrod, like Daniel Boone, had attained a wide reputation on the border as an adept backwoodsman, fur trader and surveyor. On his return trip to Kentucky, Harrod followed the north bank of the Ohio and made friends with the Delaware Native Americans. He shared their huts and food when on hunting trips in Kentucky. Despite his early negative experiences with Native Americans during the war, Harrod never developed a hatred of them. He established a reputation of generosity, often using his hunting skills to provide food for those less skilled than himself.[13]

While in the Bluegrass area, James also lived among French traders and learned to speak their language. They carried the furs down the Mississippi

A historical postcard of George Washington. *Author's collection.*

River to New Orleans because the gulf port prices were better, even though British orders were to take cargo to Fort Pitt. From there, he traveled into the areas that form present-day Kentucky and Tennessee.[14]

In the mid-1700s, Kentucky was inhabited by Native American tribes like the Shawnees, Iroquois, Delawares, Cherokees and Chickasaws. They sent hunting parties down the Ohio and Kentucky Rivers to find fresh water, abundant wildlife and rich vegetation. Very territorial, the northern tribes meticulously killed all intruders and took their land. The tribes begrudgingly shared Kentucky as a hunting ground for many years, but the peace did not last. For generations, we have heard of the "dark and bloody ground," but this is not necessarily the truth. This myth may be attributed to a statement by the Cherokee leader Dragging Canoe during the March 1775 treaty negotiations at Sycamore Shoals. Dragging Canoe reportedly said that a dark cloud hung over the land, known as the Bloody Ground. Kentucky does not mean "dark and bloody ground" in any language.[15]

Chapter 2

1773

The Western Fever

Kentucky…what lay beyond the blue haze of their ranges was a matter of much mystery and pleasing speculation.
—*R.S. Cotterill,* The History of Pioneer Kentucky

From 1750 to 1773, Kentucky was a vast wilderness under ownership of the British empire. Various explorers like James Harrod, Daniel Boone and George Rogers Clark traveled across the Allegheny Mountains from the eastern colonies, across the Cumberland Gap from the Tennessee area and by canoe and flat barge down the Ohio and Kentucky Rivers, mostly in search of furs. "To Englishmen, Kanta-Ke was like an isle in the Great Wilderness ripe for settlement, free for the taking. Or so it seemed."[16] They soon realized the treasure they had found and set about to survey and claim the precious land. They erected "improver's cabins," a square of small logs erected breast high, but not roofed or inhabited. The Native Americans took note of their presence.

During 1772, before the start of the American Revolution, many hunters, settlers and surveyors were in Kentucky. Captain Thomas Bullitt was trained as a surveyor at the College of William and Mary and worked hard to curry favor for himself with Virginia's new governor, John Murray, fourth Earl of Dunmore. Lord Dunmore appointed Bullitt as Virginia's chief surveyor. In December 1771, Lord Dunmore allowed Captain Bullitt, thirty-eight years old, to advertise an expedition to Kentucky the next year to make surveys for military land warrants. These land warrants were first offered as an incentive to serve in the military and later as a reward for service.[17]

Oil portrait of John Murray, Fourth Earl of Dunmore by Sir Joshua Reynolds.

Grave site of Thomas Bullitt in Charleston, West Virginia. *Ryan David Schweitzer.*

Physical entrance into Kentucky was by no means easy, and there were two feasible routes from the east. One was the Ohio River in the north, and the other was the Cumberland Gap in the extreme southeast. The Ohio River hugged the entire northern boundary of Kentucky and was formed in Western Pennsylvania by the Allegheny and the Monongahela Rivers. The Allegheny drained into the northwestern portion of Pennsylvania, and the Monongahela, flowing from the opposite direction, drained into the southwestern portion of Pennsylvania. These two rivers meet at Pittsburg, the main point of departure for those going to Kentucky from the north. It required many weeks to make the trip into Kentucky, and after the first few years, this became the chief route into the land.[18]

The Cumberland Gap in the extreme southeast corner of Kentucky formed a corner with Virginia on the boundary of Tennessee. Here the Cumberland Mountains narrowed to a single range between two valleys. The Powell River branch rose into the eastern valley of the Tennessee, and in the western valley was found at the beginning of the Cumberland River. The courses of the two rivers were parallel for quite a distance and then separated only by the single ridge of the Cumberland. This ridge was

Oil painting of Daniel Boone escorting settlers through the Cumberland Gap by artist
George Caleb Bingham.

continuous and difficult to cross except at the gap. Pioneers had to follow
the Cumberland River until it passed through the Pine Mountains into
Kentucky. This was the route taken by settlers who were mainly from the
Shenandoah and Yadkin River regions.[19]

In the spring of 1773, Harrod joined up with Captain Bullitt to survey
land at the falls of the Ohio, near present-day Louisville. They spent several
weeks in Pittsburgh at Fort Pitt burning and hollowing out logs to make
pirogues, or canoes, and lay in supplies. Because there were no forts after
they passed the upper Ohio River, Harrod's group had to make sure they
had plenty of axes, butcher knives, blankets, extra moccasins and hunting
shirts, in addition to bullets, gunpowder and fishing tackle. They also needed
surveyor's equipment, including a rod, chain and compass.[20]

A good English Sheffield scalping knife and a blacksmith-made tomahawk
were highly sought-after possession. Records dating from 1745 in Sheffield,
England, list John Barlow as a registered cutler. By 1764, Barlow's pen and
"clasp" (folding) knives, some types having two to four blades, were selling
well at home and in the colonies. Revolutionary War ads urged American
recruits to sign up and bring their guns and Barlow knives.[21]

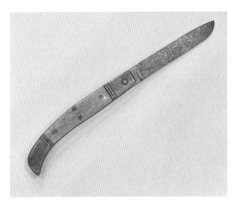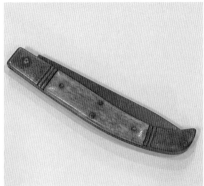

An example of a Barlow knife (open on the left; closed on the right). *Mel Stewart Hankla.*

The frontiersman's most important belongings were his axe and his rifle. An axe should have enough weight to drive deeply into the wood by its own momentum. It should be made with well-tempered steel and a uniformly sharpened cutting edge. Better yet, having two cutting edges, one for chipping and the other for brushing and rough work, was an excellent idea.[22]

Among Harrod's most prized possessions was his long rifle. Harrod's long rifle was tailor made by the old Pennsylvania Dutch and was among the longest, straightest and truest in the wilderness. Although known for years as the "Kentucky rifle," the celebrated long rifle of muzzle-loading days was developed on a Pequea Valley farm in the Mennonite region of southern Lancaster County, Pennsylvania. It was a Swiss gunsmith, Martin Meylin, who developed this new type of firearm, known as the Pennsylvania rifle.[23]

A typical Pennsylvania rifle was made for the western hunters and weighed between seven and nine pounds, with its overall length a symmetrical fifty-five inches from muzzle to butt plate. It could fire a .45-caliber lead ball from three hundred yards and kill a man or beast. Its small bore, long, heavy barrel with flint lock required only a small charge, making it exceedingly accurate. The short-muzzle European guns lacked the range for killing buffalo from two hundred yards and used more gunpowder than the Pennsylvania rifles. Later, the Pennsylvania long rifle, which eventually became known as the Kentucky long rifle, was the primary defense and hunting weapon at Old Fort Harrod.[24]

Making a rifle in the 1700s was a slow, painstaking task requiring about a week's time. The cost would vary from ten dollars to fifty dollars or more depending on the ornamentation and engraving applied to it. The early

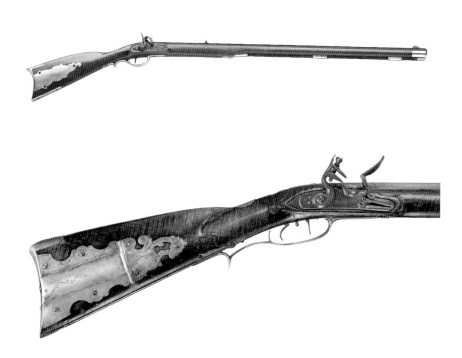

Top: A Kentucky long rifle. *Bottom*: A close-up of the stock of a Kentucky long rifle. *Mel Stewart Hankla.*

locks were entirely handmade down to the smallest screws, springs and pins. The stocks, which were made of native curly maple, were selected for the beauty of the grain. Many were embellished with intricate carved designs. Patch boxes, thimbles, trigger guards, butt plates and the various inlays that were found on the long rifles were fashioned from brass or silver and usually decorated with delicate engravings.

The barrel was the most important part of the rifle and required the most skill. Superstition dictated the welding of the barrel be done from the middle toward both ends in order to purge any devils that might be up to troublesome pranks. The barrels, which were forged from iron bars in charcoal fires, were later placed on primitive wooden rifling machines for cutting spiral grooves into the bore. The last step was browning or blacking the barrel with cider vinegar or a combination of chemicals to prevent rusting. This also lessened the chances of a rifleman betraying himself to game or enemy by reflected sunlight glinting along the barrel.[25]

Most often owners liked to express the personality of their rifle by giving it a name such as "Old Sure Fire" or "Deer Killer." In order for a rifle to continue working properly, it had to be religiously cared for. The locks had to be oiled so the hammer worked correctly, and flints had to be picked sharply. Bullets had to be filed smoothly, and the deerskin used to wrap them must be oiled so the bullets did not stick to the barrel.[26]

The term "rifle-gun" is from the eighteenth century and is helpful for making a distinction between long arms fitted with rifled barrels and smoothbore firearms. Examples of smoothbore firearms are muskets, fusils (also spelled fuse, fuzil or fuzee), fowling pieces (called "fowlers") and Indian trade-guns. Long arms were built with a rifle's more streamlined esthetics but equipped with unrifled barrels were called "smooth-rifles."[27]

Indian trade-guns in the 1770s were cheaply made smoothbore long arms. They were iron-mounted, stocked to the muzzle in walnut or maple, fitted with octagonal to round barrels up to forty-eight inches long of large caliber (sixteen to twenty gauge) and used throughout the North American fur trade. Cheaply made means that makers built Indian trade-guns to sell at a lower cost than higher-quality arms, but they were not poorly made junk pieces. Native Americans were thorough traders, and European merchants catered to their demands. Light, rugged and versatile, a smoothbore handles many types of loads—shot, ball or buck and ball.[28]

James Harrod was at least thirty-one years old when on these scouting and surveying expeditions, and he spoke the Delaware language. Harrod served as a guide to Captain Bullitt, who had just come from Chillicothe, Ohio, where he had held council with the Shawnee Native Americans. At the mouth of the Kanawha River, Bullitt separated from the others and journeyed into the interior of the Ohio country to visit the Miami Native Americans, who, it was feared, might have a natural reluctance to see the Iroquois abandon the Kentucky lands claimed by them.[29]

It was during this expedition that James Harrod met his friend Daniel Boone near the Tennessee River, at the site of present-day Nashville. Boone had been settled in the back country of North Carolina when he developed western fever. Boone and Harrod both had nothing but praise for the abundance of forest, game and pastures in Kentucky. Contrary to popular belief, Daniel Boone never made Kentucky his permanent home, but Kentucky became James Harrod's permanent home and he stayed until his death. Thus, Kentucky and Harrodsburg can justifiably lay exclusive claim to him. The deeds of James Harrod made possible the early settlement and security of the future state of Kentucky.[30]

At this point, Lord Dunmore already owned fifty thousand acres bordering Lake Champlain—within current-day Vermont and New York—and at the New Year of 1774, he severed western Virginia's Fincastle County from Botetourt County. He hoped that this would expand Fincastle's borders into Kentucky. Colonel William Preston, the official surveyor of Fincastle County, sent three deputy surveyors to the west: Hancock Taylor, James Douglas and John Floyd. Colonel Evan Shelby was pleased with Preston's decision because he promoted Captain Bullitt's vision for Kentucky.[31]

Harrod was not an educated man by standards of formal schooling, but he was known to have kept written records and possessed books in his house. The defects of his education were supplemented by his natural talents and abilities. During this period in history, the cultivation of the intellect was deemed impracticable compared to the discipline of the body. James Harrod was also a man of great sympathy, noticeable in his attention to the safety and wants of his companions. Many an evening, he lifted the large cedar horn and sounded the warning that Native Americans had been sighted.

Harrod was an expert in the use of a rifle, a successful hunter and a skillful and dangerous adversary of the Native American. He was a feared and deadly enemy to them, yet he was highly respected by them, being the warrior and advocate he had become. Because of his charismatic demeanor, Harrod was able to find eager, land-hungry men who were dreaming of new frontiers in rich, unclaimed country below the Ohio River.

Although the Bullitt and Harrod party did not know it, the McAfee brothers—Robert, William, James and George—from Botetourt County, Virginia, had also set out to survey lands in Kentucky. The two groups unexpectedly reached the mouth of the Kanawha River, in West Virginia, at the same time. After two days of discussion, they joined forces, choosing Bullitt as their commander.[32]

Captain Bullitt's first decision was to travel into Shawnee territory and try to win the friendship of the Native Americans. Three men volunteered to go with Bullitt, as well as two passing Delaware Native Americans who were returning from a hunting trip in Kentucky. Harrod and the others were to continue on as far as the area of present-day Scioto County, Ohio.

Harrod and the McAfee brothers later learned what a risk this was for Bullitt. When he suddenly appeared at the Shawnee camp, the Native Americans were so surprised that they locked Bullitt's party up in the night until they could decide what to do. The next day, Bullitt said that more than one hundred painted Native Americans approached the jail whooping and waving tomahawks. He thought they were about to be scalped, but instead they were led into the council house. Bullitt was ordered to make a speech.

When Bullitt recovered from his shock, he explained that he and his people wanted "to settle the country on the Ohio as low as the Falls." He also added that they wanted to live in friendship with the Native Americans. To alleviate the Shawnees' fears of increased hunting in Kentucky, Bullitt said that the white men would not interfere and that they wanted to live "as brothers and friends." Chief Cornstalk agreed to give their proposal consideration and assured Bullitt that he was among brothers. Bullitt and the others were released to continue on their journey.[33]

Eventually, Bullitt and Harrod reconnected, and everyone arrived in Scioto. They proceeded down the Ohio River, allowing hunters to procure meat along the way. All was going well until one night Bullitt's surveyors boasted of their plans to lay out their plots in squares with no space between them. The McAfees argued that they had no interest in Ohio bottom land. They wanted land with small streams and good springs so they could build mills.

Bullitt did not agree and told Harrod and the other surveyors to proceed with the original plan. The surveying continued, and the McAfees remained quiet. On July 4, they camped at Big Bone Lick and were surprised at the large mastodon bones on the ground and sticking out of the marshy salt lick. One McAfee noted in his journal that the teeth of the animals must have weighed ten pounds each, the thigh bones were four to five feet long and the ribs were three to four inches wide. They used the ribs of the mastodons for tent poles and the heads for chairs. They puzzled over the mighty skeletons scattered around the spring, wondering over what sort of elephant or animal they belonged to. A Delaware Indian appeared at their camp and said that when he was a young boy, the bones were just as they saw them. The men were also amazed at the thousands of animals gathered at the salt lick.[34]

The rich salt veins underneath Kentucky's sandstone base once resulted in numerous collections of salt licks—extensive ranges of salt-laden soil surrounding springs—that drew animal herds even in the prehistoric day of the great mammals. In addition to its medicinal uses, settlers used salt as a preservative. Little wonder that Harrod and his men risked their lives to render salt, even during times of heavy Indian attacks.[35]

On July 7, the two groups split up again, and each began its own surveying. Harrod stayed with Bullitt, and on July 8, they reached the falls of the Ohio

The entrance sign to Big Bone Lick State Historic Site. *Keith Rightmyer.*

and began to lay out a town at what is present-day Louisville. The McAfee party left Bullitt and his company and followed a buffalo trace down the Ohio River to reach the mouth of the Kentucky and present-day Frankfort. They decided that they did not like the site for a permanent settlement, so they rowed up the river twenty miles until they came to a salt lick where they went ashore to get a view of the game roaming there. They called the salt lick Drennon's, for one of the men in their company. They continued to travel on until they reached the banks of the crooked Salt River, and here is where they made extensive surveys.[36]

By late summer, Harrod was continuing on down the Kentucky River to scout for his own settlement on what he thought was the best land in Kentucky. The Native Americans called the Kentucky Bluegrass Region the "Great Meadow" because of the tall grass and thick canes. Unbeknownst to each other, Harrod and the McAfees had chosen almost identical locations for their settlements.[37]

When preliminary scouting and surveying was complete, Harrod returned home to North Carolina to talk his plans over with his elder brother, Thomas. The people of Virginia and North Carolina were all nursing "Kentucky fever." Pioneers were busy with plans to move "where the buffalo were too fat and lazy to run from the rifle shot and the thick rich cane growth offered perfect pastures for horses and cattle."[38]

During the late summer of 1773, Chief Cornstalk broke the uneasy truce and directed a massacre of families on the Greenbriar and other outlying stations. This is about the same time Daniel Boone had decided to move his family from the Yadkin Valley of North Carolina to Kentucky. On September 25, 1773, the Boones and five other families set out, and upon reaching Wolf Hills at present-day Abingdon, Daniel dispatched his seventeen-year-old son, Jamie, and several others to Russell's Fort to retrieve supplies. On October 9, Jamie and his group were attacked by bands of Delawares, Shawnees and Cherokees.

Because of the Treaty of Fort Stanwix, Native Americans in the region were trying to figure out what to do about all the settlers entering the territory. This group of Native Americans decided to send a message of their opposition to settlers. Jamie Boone was captured and gruesomely tortured to death. The brutality of the killings sent shock waves along the frontier, and Boone's party abandoned its expedition.[39]

Harrod was not going to let the Native Americans prevent him from returning to Kentucky. As he continued on with his plans, Colonel William Preston, surveyor of Fincastle County, refused to enter any of Captain Bullitt's surveys. Preston said that Bullitt refused to hire Fincastle deputy surveyors as required by Virginia law and that he had staked his surveys in Shawnee land under treaty to the Crown. Bullitt also failed to tip Preston a little gratuity for his trouble in overseeing Fincastle's disputable claims. Colonel Preston demanded Bullitt's surveys had to be redone under his supervision, and he doubted that the men had a legal right to survey below the Kentucky River.[40]

Although Colonel Preston complained about the law violations he thought were occurring, Lord Dunmore ordered him to register the falls of the Ohio surveys in Fincastle records. In December 1773, Lord Dunmore authorized military warrants to be located anywhere in Virginia territory.[41]

Harrod did not let this bother him because he believed in the Fort Stanwix Treaty and the Virginia charter claims. He didn't care what British officials had to say, as he expected to go out, maintain ordinary settlement rights and wait for Virginia to validate the claims.[42]

Many of the reigning Virginia men—like George Washington, Thomas Jefferson and Patrick Henry—were declaring to the Crown that they would rather die than to live under tyranny. On December 16, 1773, a

Historical postcard of the Boston Tea Party from a 1789 engraving. *Author's collection.*

Historical postcard of the Boston Tea Party from the 1846 print by Nathaniel Currier. *Author's collection.*

most powerful protest was happening in Boston. The protest took place at night and was extremely silent, lasting only three hours. There were no women participating, only men, and most of them in their teens. They came in disguise because to be caught would mean arrest and jail. The protestors boarded three ships in Boston Harbor and threw 342 chests of tea overboard. The Boston Tea Party led to the birth of a new country.[43]

Chapter 3

1774

First Permanent Settlement West of the Allegheny Mountains

The town thus laid off was named Harrodstown, and subsequently known or spoken of as Oldtown, even for years after it received its present name of Harrodsburg.
—*Lewis Collins,* Collins' Historical Sketches of Kentucky: History of Kentucky, *vol. 2*

In the 1700s, the Native American tribes who hunted in Kentucky included the Cherokees, Delawares, Wyandottes, Iroquois and Shawnees. The Shawnee Nation was the most neglected and unfortunate tribe of the whole region of the Ohio Valley and the Great Lakes because its members were too remote for the French in Louisiana to benefit by their trade.[44]

In March 1774, James Harrod was ordered by Lord Dunmore to lead an expedition to survey the bounds of land promised by the British Crown to soldiers who served in the French and Indian War. The Allegheny Mountains were a great incentive to the imagination of the frontiersman. James Harrod, with John Cowan as his second in command, and thirty-one brave men came from Virginia and assembled at Graves Creek before moving down the Monongahela River to the Ohio River into Kentucky. Harrod led his men three hundred miles beyond the farthest outpost, west of the Kentucky River and on land specifically designated by treaty as belonging to the Native Americans.[45]

James Harrod was elected captain of the expedition, and this company consisted of the following men:

Blackford, Joseph, PA
Blair, James, PA
Brown, James, PA
Brown, John, PA
Campbell, Arthur, VA
Campbell, William, VA
Chaplin, Abraham, VA
Clark, John, VA
Cowan, Jared, PA
Crawford, John, PA
Crow, John, VA
Crow, William, VA
Davis, Azariah (Annanias), VA
Davis, James, VA
Doran, Patrick, VA
Dugan, Henry
Fields, William, VA
Garrett, William, VA
Glenn, David, PA
Glenn, Thomas, PA
Harlan, Elijah, VA
Harlan, James, VA
Harlan, Silas, VA
Harmon, John Valentine, VA
Harrod, Levi, PA
Harrod, Thomas, NC
Hinton, Evan (John?), VA
Hite, Abraham, VA
Hogan, Henry, VA
Kerr, James, PA
Martin, William, PA
Mortimer, William
Myers, William
Ooley, Peter
Poage, George, VA
Quirk, Thomas, VA
Rees, Azor (Azaria?)
Sanders, James, VA
Shelp, John, VA
Smith, John, VA
Sodowsky, James, VA
Stull, Martin, VA
Venable, William
Wiley, James, VA
Williams, David, VA
Wilson, John
Zane, Andrew, VA[46]

Amid the chilling winds of March, the tiny company traveled by canoes down the Monongahela and Ohio Rivers into the mouth of the Kentucky River. The rivers would have been running swift and high from melting snow and thawing ice. The Kentucky River led to the area becoming known as Harrod's Landing on Oregon Creek, in the lower end of present-day Mercer County and east of the village of Salvisa. They then came across Salt River near McAfee's Station, up to present-day Fountainbleu and finally to a creek, later to be known as Town Creek. They pushed on up the creek until they came to its source at the Big Spring. It was here they made camp and the eventual settlement of Harrodstown.[47]

The Town Creek, or Gore's Spring, named after Andrew Gore, who purchased it in 1815, was just 265 feet west of the old or original "Town Spring" at the northwest corner of the block of land on which the old fort stood. This old Town Spring has been dried for more than a century, and the vein that supplied it has been directed into other veins making the present Town Spring.[48]

In 1774, Kentucky was part of Virginia and under the Virginia Frontier Settlement Act. If you traveled west across the Appalachian Mountain Range to the land that is now Kentucky, you had to designate your claim by cutting your "mark" into the trees at the four corners of your land and live on it one year, or plant a corn crop on it, and then the land was yours. Harrod and his men began laying off a town on June 16, 1774, and they named it Harrodstown, which became the first permanent English settlement west of the Allegheny Mountains, later to be called Harrodsburg. The men started clearing the roads of Harrodstown on the south side of Town Creek. These extended a half mile in an east–west direction, where the road originated at a point near the Big Spring Station camp and terminated near the site where the Old Fort would later be erected in 1775–76.[49]

Daniel Boone spent the winter of 1769–70 in a cave on the waters of Shawnee Run, approximately four miles east of Harrodstown. The entrance

Historical postcard of Boone's Cave on Shawnee Run farm. *Author's collection.*

A photo of the engraving on a portion of the tree with Daniel Boone's initials, "D.B." *Old Fort Harrod State Park.*

of the cave is about twenty feet wide and eight or nine feet high. On a high bank just over the mouth of the cave is a tree that bore the initials and date "D.B. 1770." In 1775, Daniel Boone established Boonesborough. The museum at Fort Harrod has the section of the tree with "D.B. 1770."[50]

Within two weeks of Harrod's arrival, Isaac Hite and his daring band of eleven men joined Harrod at Harrodstown. Most of these men had fought in the French and Indian War. Rendezvousing near the Big Spring, east of Harrodstown, the men proceeded with great eagerness to locate and select by lot places suitable for building cabins. They also founded and claimed Fountainbleu Spring. Isaac Hite's company included:[51]

Gilbert, Robert	Petrey, Alexander
Hamilton, James	Poage, George
Hite, Isaac	Sandusky, Jacob
Knox, James	Shelp, John
McColloch, James	Sodowsky, James
Tutt, Benjamin	Williams, David[52]

The first corn crop in Kentucky was planted at Fountainbleu by David Williams, John Shelp and James Sodowsky in 1774.[53]

The following is a list of additional names of men who located land or built cabins in the vicinity of Harrodstown in the summer of 1774:

Batson, Mordecai	Hanson, Thomas
Cowan, James	McCray, Roderick
Douglas, James	Nash, William
Floyd, John	Taylor, Hancock
Hamilton, James	Taylor, Richard[54]

Harrod's men constructed temporary log and brush structures to live in while they made improvements on their land. The men divided into small companies to select locations, improve lands and drew lots scattered over a wide area from the station camp. Every man would receive two lots, one containing one and a half acres and the other ten acres. On these lots they built cabins, known as Lottery Cabins: "[T]hat a cabbin [sic] should be built each person contiguous to each other, or as much so as the situation of the country would admit. That after the cabbins were built, they should be numbered and each person to draw his lott and to possess that cabbin on which the number stood, and that the dividing line should be halfway between each cabbin."[55]

Half-acre in-lots were laid out on either side of the street, and ten-acre out-lots were on the periphery of the town and were assigned to each of the men. The men drew numbers to determine their cabins and acreage. Four or five cabins were built near the spring and several on the in-lots. Although out-lots extended north of the creek, little land was cleared as the cabins were raised.[56]

The John Crow lottery cabin was near the Town Spring of present-day Danville, James Brown's lottery cabin was on Clark's Run less than a mile southeast of the Danville spring, James Blair's was just over a mile southwest, William Field's was just over a mile west of Danville, John Crawford's was four miles south of Danville and James Wiley's was three miles east of Harrodsburg. There is good reason to believe that cabins were not built for all of the company, and therefore those built were apportioned by lot. The men of Hite's company "improved," but generally without building cabins. The Big Spring was the rallying point for Harrod's company, where they were joined by Hite's men, and they laid off the town.[57]

The state highway marker for the Big Spring. *Keith Rightmyer.*

James Harrod drew an out-lot at Boiling Spring, also known as Payne's Spring, about three miles east of Harrodstown. He proceeded to build a number of rude log cabins. Harrod built at Boiling Spring because he was guaranteed a bountiful, flowing supply of fresh water.[58]

The first fort in 1774 was three log cabins built below the Big Spring and enclosed with large "hoop poles" or sapling trees. They were sharpened at the top, and the base was firmly set in a trench that was opened up around the cabins. The poles were then securely fastened together with hickory bark, woven in and out between the poles making a stockade 7 to 8 feet high. This frail protection afforded the men some little security against prowling bears and Native Americans. They only lived here a short time, afterward building three more cabins about 285 feet from the Big Spring (East Street). They lived here while the fort was built on the high hill above Gore Spring.[59]

Soon surveyors passing through Harrodstown reported an increasing number of Indian attacks along the western borders of Virginia and Pennsylvania. The governor of Virginia, Lord Dunmore, and his agents were alleged to have incited both sides of the Native American conflict. Dunmore asked the House of Burgesses to declare a state of war with the hostile Native American nations and then ordered up an elite volunteer militia force for the campaign.[60]

On July 8, 1774, Daniel Boone and Michael Stoner were sent by Captain William Russell, per instructions of Colonel William Preston, the military commander of Fincastle County Virginia, to notify Harrod and the other white men of the increasing Indian hostilities. Scouts were also sent out because of fears the Cherokee would combine with the northern Native Americans. Russell wrote, "I am in hopes, that in two or three weeks from this time Mr. Boone will produce the gentlemen surveyors here, as I can't believe they are all killed. Boone has instructions to take different routes till he comes to the Falls of the Ohio and if no discovery there, to return home through the Cumberland Gap…if they are alive, it is indisputable, but Boone must find them."[61]

A drawing of the Big Spring settlement by Ruth Beall (1913–2002) as the area appeared in 1774. *From* Harrodsburg *(Images of America series).*

The Big Spring as it currently appears. The area has been turned into a small park with a walking trail. *Keith Rightmyer.*

A historical postcard of the Falls of Ohio. *Author's collection.*

Boone and Stoner began their journey from the Clinch Valley and lost no time in reaching Kentucky. On this trip, Boone passed over the site of the future Boonesborough. They reached Harrodstown in the middle of the building activity. After a few days' delay, the two messengers proceeded to the falls of the Ohio to warn the men there. They reached home by way of the Cumberland Gap sixty-eight days after they had left, traveling more than eight hundred miles on their journey.[62]

When James Cowan was killed on July 26, 1774, George Poague, who came to Kentucky with Harrod, was in the party at Fountainbleu. Poague was a nephew of Colonel William Poague, and when Native Americans fired on the party, Cowan was killed. The rest of the party ran, but two Native Americans chased Poague. Poague had his gun in his hand but was so closely pursued that he had no time to turn and shoot. The natives were so near that they tried to seize his gun, but Poague threw his gun to one side. The Native Americans grabbed the gun and fired at Poague with his own gun. Fortunately, they missed. He escaped to Harrodsburg.[63]

Shortly after Boone came through Harrodstown, on July 20, 1774, a party of men was ambushed near a Mercer County spring. Two of the men, while separated from the others, were surrounded and killed. Two of the others escaped but headed straight back to their homes in Virginia with nothing but the clothes on their back. A fourth man, John Harmon, reached Harrodstown and reported the news.[64]

Harrod and his men left to join the campaign to defend the western border of Virginia. The conflict resulted from escalating violence between British colonists—who in accordance with previous treaties (1768's Treaty of Hard Labor and Treaty of Fort Stanwix)—were exploring and moving into land south of the Ohio River, modern West Virginia and Kentucky, and the Native Americans, who held treaty rights to hunt there. Harrod and twenty-seven men joined the Fincastle Battalion under the command of Colonel Christian's regiment and went on to the Point Pleasant campaign but arrived too late to participate in the war's only major battle. The Battle of Point Pleasant, now officially recognized as the first battle of the Revolutionary War, ended on October 10, 1774.[65]

Along the Ohio River near modern Point Pleasant, West Virginia, Native Americans under Shawnee chief Cornstalk attacked Virginia militia under Colonel Andrew Lewis, hoping to halt Lewis's advance into the Ohio Valley. After a long and furious battle, Cornstalk retreated. The Virginians, along with a second force led by Lord Dunmore, marched into the Ohio Valley and compelled Cornstalk to agree to a treaty, ending the war. By their treaty, the Native Americans pledged not to cross the south of the Ohio except for trade and to do no harm to white men coming down the river. History shows that the war was provoked more by white men

A photo of the current Fort Randolph at Point Pleasant. *Photo by Kevin Myers.*

Left: A 1915 painting is based on a black-and-white engraving published by Benson John Lossing in 1868.

Opposite: The state highway marker for McAfee Station. *Keith Rightmyer*.

than by Native Americans and became known as Lord Dunmore's War, a name given to it in commemoration of its chief provoker.[66]

The Virginians lost about 75 men, with 140 wounded. The Shawnees' losses could not be determined since they carried away their wounded and threw many of the dead into the river. The next morning, Colonel Christian, who had arrived shortly after the battle, marched his men over the battlefield. They found 21 dead braves in the open, and 12 more were discovered hastily covered with brush and old logs. Among those killed was Pucksinwah, the father of Tecumseh.[67]

After Dunmore's War, the whole country was "ringing from one end to the other of the beautiful Kentucky and the banks of the pleasant Ohio." According to the *Draper Collection*, "Those who have been there gave the most enticing accounts of its beauty, fertility, and abundance of game. The Buffalo, Elk, and Bear were said to be rolling fat, and weary for the rifle shot."[68]

Harrod's men had done most of their surveying south of the McAfee brothers' claims, but there was a sufficient overlapping to necessitate a general discussion and some individual bargaining to come to a preliminary agreement; the two parties settled down to work in general harmony. Although they straightened out most of the conflicts, it was many years before the courts settled the last land claims.[69]

The McAfee brothers were also early settlers in Kentucky and had made explorations during 1773 and 1774. Robert B. McAfee wrote in his journal that "the…McAfee Company…intended to return to Kentucky to improve and look after their lands, [near present-day Salvisa, at a place called Oregon] but previous to their getting ready to start, hostilities broke out." The brothers returned to their claims after Dunmore's War.[70]

Chapter 4

1775

THE TRANSYLVANIA COMPANY

A richer and more beautiful country than this [Kentucky],
I believe has never been seen in America yet.
—*Lowell H. Harrison and James C. Klotter,* A New History of Kentucky

In October 1774, Lord Dunmore and the Shawnee Native Americans signed the Treaty of Camp Charlotte in Scioto, Ohio. By the terms of the treaty, the Shawnees agreed to give up the land rights and cease hunting south of the Ohio and to allow boats to travel undisturbed on the river. The Native Americans also promised to return captives, slaves, horses and valuable goods.[71]

In early 1775, much of the activity in Kentucky was done by surveyors who were preparing the way for settlers. Because of this, there were also endless lawsuits over land claims and grants. This scramble for establishing land grants involved not only individuals but also larger land companies. Virginia's land agreement allowed for claims to be selected and occupied before any official surveying was complete. This system quickly brought money into Virginia's treasury, but it led to overlapping claims, boundary disputes and occasional violence between rival claimants.[72]

After Daniel Boone left Kentucky in late 1774, there was a scramble to settle. Unfortunately, some of these men were of a more hardnosed profession than the hunters and adventurers who preceded them. These were the surveyors, and they were sent by the State of Virginia. These men traveled up and down Kentucky, surveying the lands and laying out towns and cities in almost every valley. They were practical men and were concerned primarily with the land and its fertility—the beautiful forest, the wide plains and the plentiful game meant little to them. They formed the battle line for actual settlers who came into Kentucky.[73]

On March 8, 1775, Harrod led a group of forty or more men back to Harrodstown to stay at the first permanent English settlement west of the Allegheny Mountains. Flooding had ruined many of the structures built the previous summer, and the land was soaked, so these cabins were abandoned and the decision was made to construct a log fort on the hill west of the Big Spring. The site of the fort, to be started later in the summer, had been chosen by Harrod because it had several good springs and good view of the townsite and the adjoining countryside.

In March 1775, Judge Richard Henderson, from North Carolina, and his associates established the Transylvania Company and negotiated the Treaty of Sycamore Shoals with the Cherokee Native Americans. Henderson was an important man in the east—a colonel in the militia, a noted orator, a judge and a self-made man who had dreams of a great fortune in the west. He had a vision of taking over Kentucky and making it a separate country with himself as supreme ruler, or at least a new colony with himself as governor. When trying to describe the glory and bounty of Kentucky, Henderson said, "A description of the country is a vain attempt, there being nothing else to compare with it, and therefore could be only known to those who visit it."[74]

The treaty was not really a treaty but rather a deed—a purchase clearly in violation of the Royal Proclamation of 1763, which forbade private persons from engaging in land deals with the Native Americans. The company received some 200,000 acres of land lying roughly in the area bounded by the Kentucky, Cumberland and Ohio Rivers. Henderson paid $10,000 in guns and other provisions for the land; however, the Cherokees did not mention that they didn't own the land. Henderson's ambitions precluded subservience to Virginia authorities.[75]

The Royal Proclamation of 1763 was issued on October 7, 1763, by King George III after Great Britain acquired French territory in North America after the end of the French and Indian War. This order forbade all settlements west the Appalachian Mountains and rendered worthless land grants given by the British government to Americans who fought for the Crown against France. The Proclamation angered settlers who wanted to continue their westward expansion into new farmlands and wanted to keep their control of local government.[76]

No sooner had word of the Treaty of Sycamore Shoals reached Williamsburg than Governor Josiah Martin issued a proclamation strictly charging all justices of the peace, sheriffs and other officers, civil and military, to prevent the "illegal designs" of Henderson, pointing out that the king would not sanction any arrangement where Native Americans gave land titles to private purchases. He informed Lord Dartmouth, a British statesman, that Henderson's purchase was contrary to the express words and meaning of the Royal Proclamation.[77]

Although this agreement with the Transylvania Land Company violated British law, it became the basis for the white takeover of the area. It appears that Henderson never made an actual attempt to obtain approval of the royal government for his proposed colony, although he later expressed the hope that the project would be acceptable to the king.

Daniel Boone helped set up Henderson's negotiations, perhaps for money or a promise of glory in the new regime. As he left the treaty site, Cherokee chief Dragging Canoe shook Boone's hand but said, "We have given you a fine land brother, but you will find it under a cloud and a dark and bloody ground." Boone left Sycamore Shoals with thirty men and orders from Henderson to establish the capital of his Transylvania empire and to build a road through the Cumberland Gap.[78]

Boone and his men reached the banks of the Kentucky on the first of April 1775 and lost no time in clearing the land in anticipation of erecting a fort; it would be only twenty-two miles from Harrodstown, as the crow flies. Boone had built his cabin on the west bank of a little stream that flows into the Kentucky about one-half mile below Otter Creek. Henderson found it impracticable to build cabins for his men at the same place, and after reflection, he decided to build a fort on the east, some three hundred yards away. By April 22, the fort was underway, and lots had been laid off for the men.[79]

The construction of a fort was a very important factor in the life of a growing town because the Native Americans were so troublesome that the inhabitants of many towns were prevented from building cabins as provided by law. They were compelled to ask the legislature for an act extending the time for the work. The act was written in the following terms: "Whereas it is represented that the hostilities of the Indian Tribes and other causes have prevented or will prevent many of the possessors of lots in the town… of Harrodsburg in the County of Mercer and of Louisville in the County of Jefferson, from building thereon, in pursuance of the Acts by which the said towns were established. Be it Enacted By the General Assembly that every possessor of a lot in any of the said towns shall be allowed

An illustration of Dragging Canoe, played by reenactor Ron Pinson, by Dann Jacobus. *From the* Valley River Press.

the further space of three years after the day limited by law shall expire for building thereon, conformably to the Acts for establishing the said towns respectively."[80]

Boone and Henderson appeared to have selected an unsuitable place for their settlement. Boone designed to build the town in the narrow valley that lay along the banks of the Kentucky River. On the north side ran the narrow current of the stream, on whose northern banks were high cliff palisades. Settlers soon realized that from these summits a rifleman could control any point in the valley across the river. Both banks of the river were thickly screened by the trees, and these were never cut even though they provided an easy approach to the fort. On the south side, lofty hills ascended close to the fort and also commanded a security risk to the fort. On all sides the fort lay exposed to any enemy of determination and skill.[81]

Contrary to the site, speed apparently was the order of the day, and Fort Boonesborough, the first fort in Kentucky, was completed on June

An early sketch of Fort Boonesborough by George Washington Ranck (1901).

14, 1775. Toward the end of this year, there were quite a few newcomers arriving in Kentucky, and some of them located at Boonesborough. This year was also noted for the activities of Colonel Richard Henderson and his Transylvania Colony; Richardson issued a proclamation appointing a meeting at the fort for the purpose of furthering his pet scheme of forming a state. Henderson opened a land office at the Boonesborough Fort, and he had many transactions with the settlers, who lived to regret the day they had invested in real estate.

Following their treaty purchase, Henderson and his men wasted no time in starting out to claim their newly acquired land. They did not get far before realizing that the Transylvania Company's track would not permit wagon travel. It was hard for men on horses to get through the spring mires, the swollen streams, steep hill climbs and rock faces on the Wilderness Road. They ended up storing their wagons and most of the goods at Martin's Station, packed what they could hold on to while riding horses and started for the Cumberland Gap.[82]

It was here that Henderson learned from settlers returning from Kentucky about increasing Indian attacks. The surveying parties and land speculators who rushed to the west, eager to claim land under the military warrants, had threatened the northern Native Americans and sent them on the warpath.

However, the Native Americans were not raiding the settlements but rather attacking isolated surveyors who came too close to war roads or main streams.

Henderson had to move fast in establishing his settlements before the Native Americans could drive him out. He recorded in his journal that he was afraid his experiment would be wrecked at the onset. He also worried about James Harrod. Henderson could not risk an open argument with Harrod—he must and would win his support.[83]

There can be little doubt that Henderson and his partners were greatly concerned about the settlers who had come to Kentucky on the "invitation" of Captain Harrod. Henderson wrote:

> *These men got possession* [of our land] *some time before we got there, and I could not certainly learn on what terms or pretense they meant to hold land and was doubtful that so large a body of lawless people from habit and education would give us great trouble and require the utmost exertion of our abilities to manage them and not without considerable anxiety and some fear.* [Another concern was that Harrod's men] *had not contented themselves with the choice of one tract of land apiece but had made it their entire business to ride through the country marking every piece of land they thought proper, built cabins, or rather pig pens to make their claims notorious…without actually putting more than a total of three acres under cultivation.*[84]

In addition to problems with Henderson, James Harrod had another challenger. Colonel Thomas Slaughter brought a party of land seekers from North Carolina to Harrodstown. Upon their arrival, Harrod greeted them warmly and sent the newcomers out to begin their search for unclaimed land. When they realized that Harrod's men had already marked vast acreages, they began to grumble and accuse James of unfair tactics. Slaughter complained that Harrod's men had no right to mark every piece of land and secure all the good springs in the area.[85]

Harrod replied that his men had arrived first and had started a town. The men marking land were working for those who had returned to the settlement in order to bring out more supplies for their families. Everyone wanted good land, and Kentucky was a new country with plenty of land for all. Harrod chose his land about six miles from the settlement proper, in what is now Danville. He named his station Boiling Spring.[86]

When Henderson was visiting Harrodstown in early March, he wrote the following details in his "Expedition to Caintucky":

Monday 8th, Rainey. Was much embarrassed with a dispute between the above gentlemen [Captain Harrod and Colonel Slaughter]. *Captain Harrod with about 40 men settled on Salt River last year, was drove off—joined the army with 30 of the men being determined to live in this country had come down this Spring from Monongahela accompanied by about 50 men most of them without families.... Tho' those gents were friendly to each other and open in all their conduct they were warm advocates and champions for two different parties. A schism had raised between Harrod's men…and those from diverse parts of Virginia and elsewhere—amounting to 50 in number on both sides....Harrod's men had not contented themselves with the choice of one tract of land apiece, but had made it their entire business to ride through the country, mark every piece of land they thought proper, built cabins or rather hog pens to make their claims notorious—and by such means had secured every good spring in the country of 20 miles length and almost as broad.*[87]

By early spring 1775, buffalo were now twenty to thirty miles away, and it was harder and riskier for the pioneers to procure meat. In another journal entry from Henderson, he stated, "Tuesday 9th, We found it very difficult at first and indeed yet, to stop the great waste in killing meat. Many men were ignorant of the woods, and not skilled in hunting…would shoot, cripple and scare the game without being able to get much.…Others of wicked and wanton dispositions, would kill three, four, five, or half a dozen buffaloes, and not take half a horse load from them all."[88]

On May 7, Harrod and Slaughter came to Boonesborough to ask Henderson to settle their dispute. While Harrod and Slaughter argued, Colonel Henderson saw himself as an uneasy mediator. Henderson secretly favored Slaughter, but fearing Harrod's wrath, he refrained from voicing this conviction and tried to appear impartial. Henderson proposed that the different settlements in Kentucky should send delegates to Boonesborough on May 23, 1775, and form a representative government to make laws and rules to prevent trouble. The four distinct settlements—Boonesborough, Harrodstown, Boiling Spring Station and Logan's Station (formerly St. Asaph)—agreed to meet at Boonesborough to draw up a constitution and make laws.[89]

When the Transylvania Assembly held its meeting, it was the first American legislative assembly west of the Appalachians. The body had nowhere to house the delegates, so they found the shade of a "giant divine elm" between Boone's stockade and the unfinished Boonesborough fort as a

A sketch of the meeting of the Transylvania House of Delegates at Boonesborough in May 1775 by George Washington Ranck (1901).

suitable meeting place. This majestic tree stood on a beautiful plain, covered and perfumed by a turf of fine white clover, which made a thick carpet of green up to the trunk. It is said that between the hours of ten and two o'clock, the shade of the elm would comfortably cover one hundred people. It was a good enough place, Henderson expressed privately, for "a set of scoundrels, who scarcely believe in God or fear a devil."[90]

As the host settlement, Boonesborough was allowed six delegates; Harrodstown, Boiling Spring and Logan's Station were allowed four delegates each. Henderson explained the rights of the assembly, its policies for the colony and the procedures that were to be followed. The assembly would remain in jurisdiction of the territory, and land would be sold at company prices. The eighteen elected delegates would make up the lower house of a legislature, but the owners would constitute the upper house. Henderson would provide executive leadership, and the assembly would collect feudal-type land taxes of two shillings per one hundred acres. English common law dealing with landownership was based on the feudal system in which the monarch owned all the land but allowed favored individuals the use of it as tenants.[91]

Reverend John Lythe, a Harrodstown settler and Anglican minister, opened the meeting with a prayer. Henderson then addressed the group, calling attention to the fact that they were assembled for a worthy purpose:

You are called and assembled at this time for a noble and honorable purpose—a purpose, however ridiculous or idle it may appear at first view to superficial minds, yet it is of the most solid consequence....If any doubts remain among you with respect to the force or efficacy of whatever laws you now, or hereafter make, be pleased to consider that all power is originally in the people; therefore, make it their interest by impartial and beneficial laws, and you may be sure of their inclination to see them enforced....As it is indispensably necessary that laws should be composed for the regulation of our conduct, as we have the right to make such laws without giving offense to Great Britain, or any of the American colonies.[92]

Henderson proceeded to discuss the problem facing the new assembly. Referring to English law instead of Virginia or North Carolina law, Henderson skirted the touchy subject of prior land claims.[93] A three-man committee was formed (including Harrod), drew up a statement to acknowledge the wisdom of Henderson's reasoning and expressed an earnest desire to meet its legislative tasks. The first order of business was to draft a constitution for the new colony. Henderson wanted the constitution to have an elected assembly, with perpetual rents, and a power of veto reserved for the landowners.[94]

The convention remained in session until the twenty-seventh, and during that time it passed nine laws. These laws concerned a variety of topics: establishing courts, regulating the militia, punishing criminals, preventing profanity and Sabbath breaking, writs of attachment, clerk's and sheriff's fees, preserving the range, improving the breed of horses and, finally, preserving the game. This last law was made necessary by the fact that the abundant game of the region was already fast disappearing, owing to reckless hunting by settlers. The law for improving their horses shows that even at this date the Kentucky people were interested in the subject that later enjoyed their exclusive attention.

The delegates agreed that it was highly necessary to provide for courts, a militia, the collection of debts and the punishment of criminals. Harrod served on a number of committees, including the one on lands in which he was chairman. He drew up regulations for the militia, helped amend the bill prohibiting profane swearing and Sabbath breaking and also served on a committee with Daniel Boone for conserving game. One of his major triumphs was the law providing freedom of worship. This passed in spite of the fact that the Church of England was a state institution in Virginia. The religious provision must be accredited to the temper of the frontier delegates themselves, many of whom, like Harrod, were dissenters, Scotch-Irish Presbyterians or indifferent churchgoers.[95]

At intervals throughout their lawmaking, the legislators concerned themselves with other things. A committee was appointed to confer with Henderson concerning a suitable name for the colony; Henderson suggested "Transylvania," and the name was adopted.

Another committee, consisting of Boone and Harrod, was appointed to urge the company to grant no land to newcomers except on the conditions of higher prices than the original settlers paid. Harrod's presence on this committee was significant because he would later change his attitude entirely. Before the convention adjourned, Henderson, inviting open investigation, appeared before the body and displayed the deed the Native Americans had given him at Watauga. On the last day of the session, he entered into a written agreement with the people. By the provisions of this contract, delegates were to be elected and meet annually, judges were to be appointed by the proprietors but answerable to the people, all civil and military officers were to be appointed by the proprietors, there should be a surveyor-general who should not be a partner in the purchase and the legislative authority thereafter should consist of the delegates, a council of twelve men and the landowners.[96]

The assembly agreed to meet again in September 1775, and the delegates adjourned. The settlers returned to their surveying, clearing and planting. In Harrodstown, they erected more cabins around the Town Creek, chinked the older buildings and worked on construction of Fort Harrod. By the end of summer, Harrodstown boasted a seventy-acre cornfield and eight to ten cabins.[97]

During Harrod's years in Kentucky, his first loyalty was to the men who had chosen him as their leader. However, some of his men were unwilling to obey what they considered unnecessary and arbitrary restrictions on their movements. Newcomers, seeing the muddled state of affairs in the Transylvania Colony, choose to ignore the rulings or returned to their old homes in the east rather than risk their efforts on uncertain claims.[98]

On June 14, 1775, Harrod was solicited by James Nourse and Benjamin Johnson to act as a land locator. After purchasing some horses, the men met Harrod at Boiling Spring and from there traveled to Boonesborough by way of Knob Lick and Twitty's Fort. The men crossed the river into Fincastle County, Virginia, and continued northward to the waters of the Licking River, where they made several surveys. Because none of these men was an official deputy surveyor, their trip was a waste of time and their unauthorized surveys illegal. Their guide, Harrod, was not at all familiar with the area and was uncertain whether he was on the waters of Eagle Creek or the Licking River.[99]

Kentucky was fast becoming a white man's land. Henderson opened a land office at Boonesborough and was granting land to actual settlers. He had also made out commissions for local officers at Logan's Station, Boiling Spring and Harrodstown. He had taken occasion to personally visit the three forts and found with a degree of pleasure that although provisions, especially salt, were scarce, the people seemed prosperous and well pleased with Kentucky and the company.[100]

The settlers were running short of flour and suffered from lack of greens until the vegetable patches began to mature. The Transylvania proprietors provided ammunition for the men but could help little with other needed articles because of their inability to bring out the bulk of provisions they had packed in the wagons, still on the other side of the Wilderness Road pass.

When Henderson had opened the earlier convention, he bowed to the attentiveness of Virginia's royal governor, but he then went calmly on with his own undertakings. However, some of the settlers were having a different effect on the proclamation, especially over at Harrodstown and Boiling Spring, where Captain Harrod's influence was prevailing and disillusionment began to appear. Harrod had been hoping to secure political privileges and large tracts of land for himself, and his friends had induced his supporters to send a letter of protest.[101]

The revolt coming to light at Harrodstown was very natural because the site had been settled long before Boonesborough, and the settlers were not pleased to be thrust in the background while a later settlement secured and enjoyed the honor of being the capital. Isaac Hite was the leader in this movement. This ill feeling between the two towns was heightened by the fact that the Boonesborough people were Carolinians and Harrodstown people were Virginians. The settlers of Harrodstown had made their claims under Virginia government and did not enjoy the prospect of exchanging the rule of the state for the specific regulations of the Transylvania Company. Land was cheaper under Virginia land laws than under Transylvania laws.[102]

Others came to the west that summer, and more and more turned to Harrod for authority, leaving Henderson in a depressed state of mind. Finally, disheartened and ignored, Henderson returned to North Carolina for consultation with his co-proprietors, who, to worsen matters, were quarrelling among themselves.

The Transylvania Company voted to give Daniel Boone two thousand acres of land for his "signal services" to the company. At this time, there was an announced increase in land prices from twenty shillings to two pounds, ten shillings per one hundred acres. Joining Daniel Boone on his second expedition to Boonesborough was a hot-tempered, loud-talking but able Scotch-Irishman named Hugh McGary. After passing through the Cumberland Gap, McGary finally settled himself and his new family near Harrodstown in September 1775.[103]

The cabins built at in Harrodstown in 1774 were along the branch of the Town Creek on the low ground. When Hugh McGary's party arrived in September 1775, they selected an eminence about three hundred yards farther west as a more suitable location, on account of a spring issuing from the foot of a rocky bluff on the north side. There McGary, Denton, Harrod and three others had originally erected cabins; when the Poage party arrived in February 1776, Hugh Wilson's was the only family residing in the old cabins.[104]

The Kentucky settlers could plow the ground, fence in new clearings and erect cabins, but only the arrival of women and children could give stability to the settlements. The women and children began arriving in September 1775. There was also resurgence in the work of completing the fort, which the increasing number of the Native American attacks rendered a necessity. The construction on the stockade began, and it was completed by early spring. The fort enclosed an area of about one and a half acres, with a spring and a stream running through for fresh water. Settlers were warned of an Indian attack by a large cedar horn sounded from the fort. Fort Harrod was a defensive, arsenal fortification, and its walls served as a stronghold ready to protect settlers living on the outside. It became an important haven to the pioneers of Kentucky—as the American Revolution intensified, the British encouraged the Native Americans to raid the Kentucky settlements.[105]

Harrodstown had lush grass and abundant water, and the limestone soil made it a pastureland for grass-eating animals that was without parallel in pioneer history. Bears provided an excellent meat substitute for bacon. Game was plentiful, but so were Indian raids. The new fort was nearly completed and conveniently located; it provided refuge for both the people of Harrodstown and other settlers when the Native Americans were on the warpath. The fort of 1775–76 was located about one-half mile below the Big Spring and was built on higher ground than the 1774 Big Spring's encampment.[106]

The higher ground allowed an unobstructed view in all directions. There were numerous springs at the newer site, with a natural spring being located within the walls of the fort. This spring was a primary water source for the people of the fort and always supplied them with a constant water supply. Even while being attacked by Native Americans, drinking water could be obtained in relative safety. The fort never fell to an enemy.

A photo of the replica of Old Fort Harrod. *Keith Rightmyer*.

Fort Harrod was built of hand-hewn logs ten to twelve feet tall in a "parallelogram" configuration measuring 264 feet by 264 feet. Thousands of trees were cut and the bark peeled off. The bark had to be removed because it made the fort more prone to fires set by the Native Americans. The logs of the 10-foot-high stockade were embedded in a trench and were pointed to make notches in which riflemen on the fire walk could rest gun barrels and fire without being seen from outside. First, the base wall was built with a blockhouse on each end. On the south side of the fort, the cabins' walls formed the actual stockade wall. The chimneys were kept inside the walls so Native Americans could not stop them up. Then the three remaining walls and the blockhouses on each corner were built.

Blockhouses were not only military centers but also leader's dwellings. Their ample size also sheltered families in times of danger. At this time, the Fort Harrod community population of about two hundred included thirty-seven outlying farm families, who lived in the fort only when under Native American attack. The farmers planted seeds they brought from the east and ate the game and wild fruit of the new frontier. According to an interview by John Shane in Bath County in May 1841, Josiah Collins claimed that he cut down the first tree for the fort, which was a burr oak about two feet across at the bottom and stood near the spring, and this log was said to be used on the lower side of the first blockhouse.[107]

The log houses of Fort Harrod consisted of one room with a dirt floor and were approximately twenty feet by twenty feet. Some cabins had a loft that could be reached by a ladder for sleeping. The first-floor room usually had a rope bed, crude table and chairs for eating and a fireplace for heat, light and cooking, with cooking utensils hanging from it. The fort's cabins, three blockhouses and schoolhouse were of foot-thick logs squared on the top and bottom to fit snugly when chinked with clay and straw.

The blockhouses measured about twenty-five feet by forty-four feet. Only three of the planned four blockhouses were ever built at Fort Harrod. The northwest blockhouse was never built because of a large freshwater spring located in the corner of the fort. The southwest blockhouse was the home of James Harrod. The southeast blockhouse was the Kentucky home and office of famed pioneer and explorer George Rogers Clark. The northeast blockhouse was home to a true pioneer lady, Anne McGinty.[108]

The blockhouses were the main defense system of the fort. Each contained two levels with five or more gun ports on each wall, from which the pioneers fired their rifles. They overhung the fort wall by about two feet on both sides, and in the overhang, they placed a trapdoor. From the blockhouses, the defenders could shoot attackers off the stockades if they got too close or tried to climb the walls. Also, the trapdoors were used to pour water down to put out fires set by the Native Americans or to drop boiling water or animal fat down on attacking Native Americans who had gotten too close to the wall to shoot from the stockades or blockhouse gun ports. Long poles were used to push hostiles back off the walls and roofs.[109]

The stockades had scaffolds from which one could fire down from the top of the walls with gates on the north and west side. The gates were two-part folding gates made of the sturdiest logs available, all about ten feet in

A historical postcard of the George Rogers Clark blockhouse at Old Fort Harrod State Park. *Author's collection.*

This page, top: A historical postcard of the Ann McGinty blockhouse at Old Fort Harrod State Park. This postcard is incorrectly labeled the James Harrod blockhouse. *Author's collection.*

This page, bottom: A historical postcard of the James Harrod blockhouse at Old Fort Harrod State Park. *Author's collection.*

Opposite: The magazine for gunpowder at Old Fort Harrod State Park. *Keith Rightmyer.*

length. A heavier gate was made and placed over the main gate to secure it better during times of Native American attacks. Once the fort gates were locked, they were not opened until the attack was over. If you got caught outside the gates during the attack, well, your scalpless body might be found there after the attack. The water source, animals and horses were housed inside the fort walls.

It took about five months to build the fort. At its height, Fort Harrod contained about eighteen cabins. The cabins were built of notched logs that had to be "chinked," which is where mud mortar and wood chips were put into the cracks between the logs. The first floors were hard-packed dirt, but hewn logs would be used later, although they were notorious for painful splinters. Every cabin had a huge stone fireplace. The first chimneys were made of wood, which proved unsatisfactory because they caught fire. Later, they were made of stone like the fireplace.[110]

The fort's gunpowder was stored in an earthen magazine camouflaged as a root cellar. The magazine had a sod roof, and the inside was lined with stone. A group of men would transport gunpowder in drum-shaped kegs that fit snugly against planks. The kegs' hoops were made of saplings rather than metal to prevent sparks. The magazine in Fort Harrod was located near the southwest corner.

A leach tub was a hopper used to leach saltpeter (potassium nitrate) from guano-heavy cave dirt or night soil dug from beneath outhouses. A V-shaped vat was built of saplings and lined with straw and twigs for filtration. Once the dirt was heaped in the tub, the maker poured water on the mix to leach from it the "mother liquor"; the leachate is a key ingredient of black powder, which consists of ten parts sulfur, fifteen parts charcoal and seventy-five parts saltpeter. Settlers also used leach tubs to leach lye from wood ashes to make soap.[111]

Without the fort, the inhabitants of Harrodstown and the surrounding country could not have existed because there was no other place of refuge accessible at the time. It was their stronghold and meeting place in time of peril. Most Kentucky pioneers, although skilled woodsmen, were farmers rather than soldiers. Their primary concern was for their families and the crops on which their survival depended. The fort was the center of all information for the development of the settlement. In it men took council together, planned for their needs and developed plans for the conquest of the great Northwest. The importance and significance of the fort cannot be overrated, and it is irrefutable proof of the resolve the pioneers had for permanency of the settlement they had founded.[112]

Harrod and his followers appealed to Virginia for help against the Native Americans and to ensure the necessary effort in defense. They also wanted to clear up the land title quarrel and make sure that Kentucky was recognized as a part of Virginia. Harrod's party called attention to the fact that Henderson's purchase conflicted with Virginia's charter rights. They pointed out that the Cherokees could have no legal basis for making the sale in the first place, since the land had already been turned over to Virginia by the Six Nations (the Iroquois) at Fort Stanwix.[113]

The Treaty of Fort Stanwix was an agreement between Native Americans and Great Britain signed in 1768 in present-day Rome, New York. The treaty established a "line of property" following the Ohio River that ceded the Kentucky portion of the Colony of Virginia to the British, as well as most of what is now West Virginia. The Kentuckians warned that should the Transylvania Company be granted title to the country, all prior claims would be invalid and the purchasers subject to almost any demand by the company. Finally, the government declared against Henderson's activities, and Transylvania, with all its brief annals, passed into history. Henderson is said to have been placated with a grant of land on the Ohio, some twelve miles square.[114]

Fort Harrod would not only be safe from flooding but would also offer protection to the settlers. It became an important haven to the pioneers of

The state highway marker for Logan's Station. *Keith Rightmyer.*

Kentucky because, as the American Revolution intensified, the British encouraged the Native Americans to raid the Kentucky settlements. The settlers at Harrodstown soon joined other pioneers in the area at Boonesborough to formulate the first regulations to govern the area.

Harrodstown was the largest fort in Kentucky at the time and had more able-bodied defenders and ammunition than St. Asaph's, also known as Logan's Station, or Boonesborough. Logan's Station was completed in 1775 on an acre of land; its walls measured 180 feet by 240 feet, with blockhouses on two corners. This station was better provisioned than Boonesborough with plenty of milk, butter and bread.[115]

No one questioned the courage or forest lore of such leaders as Daniel Boone, James Harrod and Benjamin Logan, but the situation in Kentucky demanded a different type of leader—someone with a broader strategic vision, someone not tied to a single locality, someone who could marshal the resources available in the west and wrestle some help from the government in the east. Kentucky found this leader in twenty-three-year-old George Rogers Clark. In 1775, Clark said:

> *It was at this period that I first thought of paying some attention to the interest of the country.[116]*
>
> *Harrodstown had a rough stockade. At a distance from the fort, a silent testimony of siege, the stumpy, cleared fields were overgrown with weeds, tall and rank, the corn choked. Nearer the stockade, where the keepers of the fort might venture out at times, a more orderly growth met the eye. The fort was a great parallelogram made of log cabins set end to end, their common outside wall being the wall of the fort with loopholes. At the four corners of the parallelogram the cabins jutted out, with ports in the angle in order to give a flanking fire in case the savages reached the palisade. And then there were huge log gates with watchtowers on either side, where sentries sat day and night scanning the forest line. Within the fort was a big common dotted with forest trees, where such cattle as had been saved browsed on the scanty grass. There had been but the one scrawny horse before our arrival.*

Harrod Wilson, born sometime in the fall of 1775, was the first white child born in Kentucky, but he grew up to be a worthless man. There are conflicting claims about the first white child born in Kentucky, but this was corroborated by Elizabeth Thomas and several others. Elizabeth Hays, eldest grandchild of Daniel Boone, was the first white female child born in Kentucky, at Boonesborough on June 12, 1776. William Logan, son of Benjamin Logan, was born at Harrodstown on December 8, 1776. He became a member of the convention that formed the Constitution of Kentucky in 1799. Ann Poague, daughter of William and Ann, was born in March 1777.[117]

Chapter 5

1776

CREATING KENTUCKY COUNTY

The form of jurisdiction, Clark urged, should be the sending of five hundred pounds of powder across the mountains, so that Harrodstown might defend itself against the Native Americans.
—R.S. Cotterill, The History of Pioneer Kentucky

Ammunition was needed for the defense of the settlements and acquiring wild meat for their subsistence. It was scarce, and little powder was made in the Atlantic states, although the Chiswell lead mines in Virginia were vigorously working to supply lead for the American armies and the defense of the western frontiers. The Transylvania Company had furnished much of the ammunition used the first year in Kentucky. In the spring of 1776, James Harrod and Benjamin Logan transported a quantity of lead from the Long Island of Holston, an island in the Holston River at Kingsport in eastern Tennessee, for the defense of the new country. They went on horseback, taking a packhorse and returned in twenty days with iron to defend Kentucky. Later, Harrod would successfully oppose the colonization schemes of Richard Henderson and his Transylvania Company for the area. Well respected in the settlement, Harrod would soon hold several positions of political leadership.[118]

By the late spring of 1776, the pioneer population in Kentucky was estimated to be two hundred, and most of these people were in forts at Boonesborough, Harrodstown and Logan's Station. The area north of the Kentucky River had been abandoned. John Floyd reported to William Preston in July 1776, "I think more than three hundred men have left the country since I came out and not one has arrived—except a few down the Ohio."[119]

The jurisdiction of Virginia was formally extended over the whole colony of Transylvania during 1776, to the great satisfaction of the people. Such was the first attempt to establish a privileged class and landed aristocracy in Kentucky. In the meantime, pioneer settlers were crowding into the beautiful plains on the northeast and west side of the Kentucky River, between thirty and fifty miles north of Boonesborough. They were still exploring the country, making locations and surveys and lodging in temporary camps and without families or domestic encumbrances, exposed to the incursions and depredations of the northwestern Native Americans.[120]

In February 1776, the William Poague family moved from Boonesborough to Harrodstown. James Ray came from Harrodstown to lead them. They were caught in a snowstorm. Ray killed a buffalo for meat. Later, on Gilbert's Creek of the Dicks (Dix) River, they met Samuel Coburn, James McDaniel and Julius Saunders, with their families, and they all headed to Harrodstown.[121] Dick's River is a forty-five-mile-long branch of the Kentucky River flowing through Lincoln, Boyle, Garrard and Mercer Counties. Cartographers have misspelled the river's name as "Dix" since about 1920.[122]

The Transylvania land office in late March 1776 opened an office in Harrodstown, probably designed as a conciliatory measure to accommodate the people. A Canadian Frenchman named Louis Loramie was employed by the British government as a Native American interpreter. He left Montreal and went to Detroit to stir up the Native Americans to war against the Americans, carrying out the inhuman policy of Lord Dartmouth started in 1775.[123]

In April 1776, the Harrodsburg settlers sent a petition to Virginia stating that they had incurred great expense and many hardships in settling the country. They claimed that the Transylvania Company, which had promised them an indefeasible title, had advanced the cost of the purchase price from twenty to fifty shillings sterling per one hundred acres and at the same time had increased the fees of entry and surveying at an inflated rate. They were also upset that all the Kentucky country below the mouth of the Cherokee or Hogohegee (now Tennessee River) was embraced in that cession to the Crown for a valuable consideration and that the Six Nations declared the Cherokee River to be their true southern boundary.[124]

At this time, the overflow from the Big Spring formed two small streams: the present channel, known as the Town Creek, and another branch flowing through what used to be the property of Mrs. J.P. Mitchell. In many places, traces of the bed of this stream can still be found, but the water long since ceased to flow through the Mitchell way because as the town built up, people began to dig wells and tap the underground streams, reducing the volume of water in the Big Spring. Then, too, the cutting away of the heavy timber allowed more chance for evaporation from the sun's rays, so that in time the shallower channel dried up.

In the summer of 1776, when the small party of men lived in the temporary stockade fort, the two streams were flowing. One day, they heard what they thought was the call of a wild turkey. It has been related to me that Harrod discovered the false note and said it was an Indian. So, James Ray took his gun and, as history says, "made a detour" by going up the creek that flowed through Mitchell's until he reached the spring. Finding no one, he came down the stream, following the present channel, and presently discovered the Native American hidden in the leafy branches of a three-forked sycamore tree, standing on the south bank of the creek about eighty-five yards above the fort. Ray raised his gun and shot the Native American. Ray afterward told "Uncle Jimmy" Lillard that

The James Ray tree from the book *Historical Sketch of Mercer County, Kentucky (Illustrated)* by A.B. Rue. The book was made for the Louisiana Purchase Exposition, St. Louis, in 1904. *Author's collection.*

he distinctly heard the Native American fall into the water. Lillard lived to be ninety-six years old and often repeated the story as he had heard it from Ray. Mr. Lillard died in the 1840s and is well remembered by most of our citizens of the present day.[125]

Kentucky had many charming forests and glades. The face of the country in 1776 was beautiful beyond conception. Nearly half of it was covered with cane, while between the canebrakes were frequently fine open grounds for cultivation. There was plenty of timber and extremely fertile soil producing an amazing quantity of wild grass, rye and clover. The dews were heavy, which helped the nights be cool and refreshing. There was a sure supply of sugar from the maples and a steady supply of salt from the springs. There were the screams of night birds and the squalls of wild beasts to be frequently heard. The hump of the back of the buffalo was regarded to be a great delicacy. Wild game—turkeys, deer, bear and buffalo—were eaten without bread or salt. Large crops of corn were raised in Kentucky during the 1776 growing season and generally cribbed in the fields where it was raised.[126] In the autumn of 1776, Thomas Denton would plant an acre and a half of wheat at Harrodstown, the first wheat sown in Kentucky. Denton was the brother-in-law of Hugh McGary.[127]

In 1776, Kentucky County was formed, and the fort, known as Harrod's Fort, became an organized body with laws enacted for its government. It became, so to speak, the first capital of this vast and interesting territory. In and about it gathered men of ability, energy and determination whose lives were useful to their associates and a blessing to those who came after them. They not only served their own locality well but also executed heroic service on behalf of their common country.

By June 1776, Harrod's truce with Henderson had abruptly ended, and Harrod became an outspoken opponent of the Transylvania Company. He gained followers at the other stations and forts. Henderson reported to his proprietors that "the Harrodsburg men have made a second revolt and Harrod and Jack Jones at the head of the Brigands. God knows how it may end, but things at this time bear but a dull aspect—they utterly refuse to have any land surveyed or comply with one of the office rules."[128]

Jack Gabriel Jones joined Harrod in leading the second revolt. He was a lawyer and son of a prominent Virginia family. Jones complemented abilities with Harrod's own natural leadership and charismatic abilities. Jones easily matched the Transylvania lawyers with elegant and rational arguments and knowledge of legislative methods. Later, more help came from George Rogers Clark, who had a deep interest in Kentucky.[129]

Virginia had taken no action on an earlier petition from Harrodsburg, and it was decided that Kentucky needed to have its own delegates to ensure a fair hearing. Harrod called a gathering to elect delegates to represent them in the General Assembly and to ask for separation from Fincastle County. Harrod also wanted to stop Henderson and his Cherokee land purchase, which would beat the pioneers out of their legal rights.

After a five-day election process (June 8–13, 1776), Clark and Jones were elected as the delegates. The two were instructed to appeal to Virginia to overthrow Transylvania and incorporate the country under its own government. Harrod planned two petitions to be presented at the Virginia Assembly.[130]

On June 20, a twenty-one-person general committee, the Committee of Safety, met to prepare a petition for the Virginia Convention stating their grievances. The committee included John Gabriel Jones (chairman), John Bowman, John Cowan, William Bennett, Joseph Bowman, John Crittenden, Isaac Hite, George Rogers Clark, Silas Harlan, Hugh McGary, Andrew McConnell, James Harrod, William McConnell and John Maxwell.[131]

Harrod helped the men formulate the first document as a defense of their land claims, based on bounty warrants granted by Governor Dunmore and on regular prior-occupancy laws of the colony. They claimed that Henderson's purchases were illegal on grounds that Virginia had rights to it under their charter. They stated that its citizens had "fought and bled for it," and that had it not been for the defeat of the Shawnees at the Battle of Point Pleasant, the region would still be uninhabitable. In conclusion, they asked that their delegates be recognized, stating that they had already elected a committee of twenty-one men to maintain district order.[132]

Harrod's second petition represented the new committee and drew attention to the impracticality of having only two delegates to sufficiently represent Fincastle County. He argued that it was illogical to allow the colonists to remain impartial, since a group from North Carolina was also formulating a challenge to Virginia charter rights. Harrod's name was at the top of the petition, but others were less willing to express themselves openly at this time. However, a short time later, Harrod learned that Colonel Preston had sent word that Virginia was now ready to maintain its claim against Transylvania. After this, others began to sign the petition criticizing Henderson.[133]

At this same time, Harrod was appointed to visit the northern Native Americans and find out their intentions in the war started between the colonies and England. The attitude of the Native Americans was of great importance to all of Kentucky. Everyone knew the provisions of the treaty that had closed Dunmore's War, and they also knew the extreme improbability of it being kept. Harrod had learned from a runner of the Delaware tribe on the Wabash River that the Kickapoos were ready to sign a treaty with the English.[134]

The Delawares were helpless to stop the other Indian tribes, but Harrod depended on the Delawares to safeguard the pioneers against the unfriendly tribes. If the Kickapoos joined with the British, other tribes, even the friendly Delawares, may follow. The Shawnees were already taking bribes and listening to British flattery. The Delawares declared the situation critical and suggested that "Lone Long Knife," their name for Harrod, send a reliable man to talk with the chiefs. Since he was already scheduled to head north, Harrod commissioned Garret Pendergrass, an excellent trader familiar with the northern Indian tribes, to go with him.[135]

Upon arriving at the Delaware camp, they learned the Kickapoos wanted war against the white men for stealing their favorite hunting ground. Saddened with the news, Harrod knew that there was little he could do, so he thanked his Delaware friends and left with Pendergrass to return home. Harrod knew that Kentucky needed help and quickly because the overwhelmed frontier settlements were almost out of gunpowder. They also needed to settle the question of Virginia jurisdiction in order to hope for any future assistance from the government.

The kidnapping of Jemima Boone, depicted by the Swiss painter Karl Bodmer, circa 1852.

Indian hostilities increased on July 14, 1776, when three teenage girls—Jemima Boone (thirteen) and Elizabeth (sixteen) and Frances (fourteen) Callaway—slipped away from the settlement at Boonesborough, against orders, and went canoeing on the Kentucky River. They were seized on the north shore by a small band of Cherokee and Shawnee Native Americans, and they were rushed northward. The girls tried very hard to delay their progress and began to leave signs of their route, but the trackers found the trail hard to follow and Boone feared that they were losing ground.

Betting on his woodsman skills and knowledge of Native Americans, Boone cut across the country and intercepted the trail where he hoped the Native Americans would be. On the third day, the Native Americans became complacent and halted near the Licking River to cook meat from a buffalo calf. Boone's rescue party crept up and rescued the girls, but a premature shot allowed the Native Americans to escape. The spectacular rescue of the three girls became a part of the legend of pioneer Kentucky.

Elizabeth Callaway soon married Samuel Henderson, who had been part of the rescue team. The following spring, the other two girls married young men from the rescue party. Nathaniel Hart's cabin, less than a mile from Fort Boonesborough, and his crops were destroyed during the girls' rescue.[136]

While Harrod was on his trip north, Clark and Jones departed for Williamsburg, Virginia, hoping to reach the capital before the summer session of the legislature adjourned. Their trip was rainy and miserable, and they encountered several setbacks, including scalded feet and a lost horse. Scalded feet meant that one's soles had stayed wet for so long that the many-layered, shriveled flesh peeled off in thick hunks, tearing deeply into the tender sole. For militiamen or a colonial army traveling on its feet, scalded feet could abruptly end a foray.[137] When Clark and Jones reached Fincastle County, they were disappointed to learn that the Virginia Assembly had already adjourned. Now they would have to wait until the fall session to present their petitions.[138]

At this point, Jones diverted to the settlement on the Holston, leaving Clark to proceed alone to Richmond. They didn't know that at the same time they left Harrodsburg, the Virginia Convention had taken up Kentucky's December 1775 petition and passed a resolution reaffirming significance of settlements as the source for land claims and denying the validity of titles carried by Native Americans in violation of Virginia charter. However, the convention refused an appeal by Harrod for additional pay allowances for his men who served in Dunmore's War.[139]

Clark visited the new Virginia governor, Patrick Henry, to secure his backing for the Harrodstown cause. Clark appeared before the council at Williamsburg with a letter from Governor Henry, making the executive council aware of Kentucky's shaky position and officially informing them of his support. Clark ran into opposition from several peers who did not approve of frontier expansion. After much debate and arguing that the western settlements could not survive without gunpowder, the proposal was accepted, and Clark was granted five hundred pounds of gunpowder.

On August 23, 1776, the powder was sent to Fort Pitt in Pittsburgh, to be "delivered to…George Rogers Clark, or his order, for the use of the said inhabitants of Kentucki." Clark sent a letter to Harrod to tell him to send a party to Fort Pitt to bring the powder home. Clark did not know that Harrod never received the letter.[140]

The first court in Kentucky County was held on September 2, 1776. George Rogers Clark, Isaac Hite, Benjamin Logan, Robert Todd, Richard Callaway, John Kennedy, Nathaniel Henderson, Daniel Boone, James Derchester and James Harrod were named justices of the peace. Levi Todd was appointed clerk of court.[141]

Clark remained in Williamsburg for the fall legislative session, and on the opening day, Jones joined him. They presented the two petitions to the assembly. They also requested to be seated as delegates from the Western Part of Fincastle County; the council refused to grant the request. Henderson, upset that his purchases had been voided, tried another tactic by attempting to have his claims validated under Virginia law at the expense of Harrod's company.

Thomas Slaughter, a past opponent of Harrod's, also had a petition on behalf of himself and others near Kentucky. It turned out that Slaughter not only reinforced the Harrodstown pleas but also called attention to the need for organized militia. By highlighting the danger of Native Americans, the Kentuckians showed that they would be a barricade for the older settlements in the East. This argument was a success, and the House of Delegates began considering a bill for creation of the new county.

The Indiana Company also protested Virginia's claim to the western lands, and Judge Henderson, who did not want a new county created out of his territory, lobbied hard to protect the fading prospects of the Transylvania Company. Clark and Jones did receive support from Thomas Jefferson and George Mason, strong allies with Harrodstown, and they fought valiantly to get Kentucky created as a county with its own local government. Jefferson agreed with Governor Henry about the

Above: An illustration of Fort Pitt and the village of Pittsborough (Pittsburg) in 1776.

Right: A painting of George Rogers Clark by Charles P. Filson (1860–1937). The original hangs at Carnegie Library of Steubenville, Ohio.

Transylvania-Harrodstown controversy and helped Clark successfully argue that Kentucky settlements were essential for the protection of the Virginia frontier.

Jefferson was able to bring out the bill, and after a month of arguing and closed-door maneuvers, the bill passed the House and the Senate on December 31, 1776. The legislature created Kentucky County, which included part of Virginia south and west of a line from the Ohio River below the Big Sandy River to the Laurel Ridge of North Carolina. With the creation of Kentucky County, the move was called "the political birth of Kentucky" and George Rogers Clark the "Founder of the Commonwealth."[142]

Clark and Jones finished their business in Virginia and prepared to return to Kentucky, but when a messenger from Fort Pitt reported that Harrod had not sent men to get the five hundred pounds of powder, their plans changed. Clark knew that those twenty-five kegs of gunpowder were vital to Kentucky's defense, so they set out toward Pittsburg. Once at Fort Pitt, the pair recruited a small group of men to assist them in transporting the black powder down the Ohio and then up the Kentucky River to Fort Harrod.

Unfortunately, Clark's every move was being shrewdly watched and evaluated by British and Indian enemies, but he was not to be manipulated. Clark and his men slipped out of Fort Pitt in the middle of the night and silently started their long trip down the half-frozen Ohio River with five hundred pounds of high-quality, rifle-grade gunpowder. They quickly made their way down the big river, with the success or failure of Kentucky resting squarely on their shoulders. Clark and his companions were forced to move between numerous bands of angry Native American war parties. As they neared present-day Maysville on the Kentucky shore of Limestone Creek, Clark decided that they were about to be overtaken. Unwilling to run the risk of losing his cargo, he buried the powder in several spots and continued downstream for a few miles before abandoning the boats and setting them adrift as a decoy.[143]

As they traveled on to Harrodstown, Clark and Jones came upon a cabin occupied by four men and learned that a surveying party led by John Todd was in the area. Clark went ahead to meet up with Todd and to request help with moving the powder, but they missed each other. So, Clark headed off to the nearest settlement, McClelland's Station.

In the meantime, Todd reached the cabin with Clark's men, and they united together. On Christmas Day 1776, while trying to retrieve the buried gunpowder, the group stumbled into a Shawnee ambush on Johnson's fork of the Licking River near the Lower Blue Licks. Jones and William Gradon and Joseph Rogers was taken prisoner, and Josiah Dixon went missing. On

December 29, forty to fifty Native Americans, led by Mingo warrior chief Pluggy, attacked McClelland's Fort. The fort only had twenty men, but after a few hours, the Native Americans left when Pluggy was killed. Charles White was killed, and John McClelland was critically wounded. Robert Todd (soon to be General Todd) and Edward Worthington were wounded but recovered.[144]

Todd and the others escaped and made their way to McClelland's Fort. At the same time, Clark had reached McClelland's Fort and sent a messenger to Harrodstown explaining what had happened and asking for a party to retrieve the gunpowder. When Todd reached McClelland's Fort, Clark had left to meet up with Harrod to recover the gunpowder.[145]

Simon Kenton, James Harrod, Silas Harlin, Isaac Hite, Benjamin Linn, Samuel Moore, Leonard Helm, Jacob Sodowsky, Andrew Francis, William McConnell and about twenty-five others left Harrodstown on the second of January 1777, but the records do not reveal whether they proceeded to McClelland's Station before they recovered the powder. According to Simon Kenton, "at the Blue Lick the company separated—some went the upper road [and] the rest went the road leading to the head of Lawrences Creek and the road was then well known to the company by that name."

Within a short time and without incident, the men reclaimed the powder and returned to Fort Harrod. On January 6, John McClelland died of his wounds, and about three weeks later, on January 30, George Rogers Clark escorted the widows, orphans and remaining able-bodied militiamen from McClelland's Station to Harrodstown "because of threatened Indian attack and to strengthen the remaining posts."[146]

An engraving of Simon Kenton by Richard W. Dodson. *Pennsylvania Academy of the Fine Arts.*

The brave settlers of Fort Harrod came through to save the day, retrieving the gunpowder and bringing it safely back to the fort through miles and miles of unfriendly wilderness. Once at Fort Harrod, the powder was divided and quickly distributed to the many struggling Kentucky forts and stations. This important event saved Kentucky because now the settlers could defend the forts and hunt for food. There were now 150 men fit for active duty and forty families split between Harrodstown and Boonesborough.

When Virginia created Kentucky County on December 31, 1776, Harrodstown was selected

A 2019 reenactment of the George Rogers Clark Powder Run at Old Fort Harrod State Park. *Friends of Fort Harrod.*

A 2019 reenactment of the George Rogers Clark Powder Run at Big Spring Park. *Old Fort Harrod State Park.*

An oil painting of Benjamin Logan, artist unknown, circa 1802.

as the county seat. Fort Harrod became a stockade stronghold for the pioneer families until they could settle on lands of their own and proved refuge for the settlers when Native Americans were raiding. Many famous pioneers occupied the fort at various time during its eventful years. This was also the time when Benjamin Logan pushed his settlers to complete the stockade at Logan's Station.[147]

Chapter 6

1777

Year of the Bloody Sevens

The Kentucky myth of plenty had dark shadows…with 1777
as the year of the bloody sevens.
—*James C. Klotter,* The Breckinridges of Kentucky

Along the American Revolutionary War's western front, Kentuckians also called 1777 the "Year of the Bloody Sevens." Cabins would be torched, leaving bloated, mutilated corpses of men, women and children. The nerves of the walking wounded would be frayed and ragged as they surveyed the burned crops and the slaughtered cattle, hogs and goats. Lack of food and ammunition would lead to starvation and overwhelming death.[148]

The year 1777 opened with two months of deceptive calmness. The Native Americans committed no raids and seemed to have abandoned their wrath against Kentucky. In February, Benjamin Logan moved his family back to Logan's Station and reoccupied his settlement. The pioneers began to recover their spirits and venture away from the support and protection of the stockades. Unbeknownst to them, the British governor of Canada was directing his Indian allies toward Kentucky with comprehensive instructions to destroy the settlements there.[149]

At first, the Native Americans roamed around in small war parties causing mischief and mayhem. They would set fire to a cabin in Harrodstown, disappear into the woods, only to reappear at Boonesborough and scalp a hunter. They would snatch infants from mothers at the gates of forts, and other times they would just lie in wait. The white men were also coldblooded, collecting scalps and feeding Native American bodies to their dogs thinking it would make them ferocious.[150]

Captain Hugh McGary, as chairman of the Kentucky Committee of Safety, sent a memorial to the governor and Council of Virginia dated February 27, 1777, praying for aid and relief in their distressed situation:

We are surrounded with enemies on every side; every day increases their numbers. To retreat from the place where our all is centered, would be a little preferable to death. Our fort [Harrodstown] is already filled with widows and orphans; their necessities call upon us daily for supplies. Yet all this would be tolerable could we but see the dawn of peace; but a continuance of our woes threatens us—a rueful war presents itself before us. The apprehension of an incursion the ensuring spring fills our minds with a thousand fears. The brave despise danger, even death, on their own account; it is the state of weak infancy and helpless widowhood that sets heavy on us.[151]

Around March 1, 1777, William Bush and a few others arrived from Virginia, bringing public dispatches and the military and civil commissions for the officers of Kentucky County. On March 5, the militia of Kentucky County started a regiment, with a company mustered from each settlement (Boonesborough, Harrodstown and Logan's Station), and elections for officers were held at Fort Harrod. John Bowman was elected colonel; Anthony Bledsoe lieutenant colonel (he declined to serve); George Rogers Clark major; and William and James Harrod, Benjamin Logan and John Todd captains. A later election also named Todd as county attorney and Richard Callaway as the county representative to the Virginia Assembly. Prior to this, every fort and every camp had its own selected chief, with but little order or subordination.[152]

Most of the pioneers knew that there were distressing times in store for Kentucky if the Native Americans should again take the warpath. At this time, when the Kentucky settlements were in greatest need, they were also at their weakest stage. Indian attacks and the rumors of war had at the beginning of 1777 pretty well emptied the country. Three hundred people had left Kentucky, and seven stations had been abandoned. Boonesborough, Harrodstown and Logan's Station alone survived, and the latter was temporarily abandoned in the early days of 1777. Many of the people from the abandoned forts had found refuge at Harrodstown, gaining many people from Logan's and McClelland's. There were in essence only two settlements and a possible 150 men in Kentucky. The enmity between Boonesborough and Harrodstown had not abated, but rather increased because of Virginia's action in making Harrodstown the capital of the new county; nonetheless, they knew that they had to work together in order to survive.[153]

The first two months of 1777 were sufficient for completing the military organization of the Kentucky pioneers. Colonel Bowman was to lead a regiment of troops from Virginia, and Clark, who had been commissioned major, personally commanded at Harrodstown. Captain Calloway and Captain Boone were in charge at Boonesborough, and Captain Logan was supervising at his station. Clark was in charge of the entire militia of the county until Bowman arrived in September 1777.[154]

When Shawnee chief Cornstalk was killed at the Battle of Point Pleasant, he was succeeded by Cot-ta-wa-ma-go, also known as Chief Blackfish. The first attack on March 6, 1777, on Fort Harrod was a Shawnee war party led by Chief Blackfish. They ambushed William and James Ray, stepsons of Hugh McGary, and William Coomes at their maple sugar camp near the fort. William Ray was wounded and captured, but James Ray, who possessed what were possibly the longest legs on the western continent, made his escape and ran away while the Native Americans stood dumfounded at his speed. Coomes hid in a hollow log and struggled to keep quiet as the Shawnees tortured and eventually killed William Ray. When James reached the fort, he gave the alarm, and Hugh McGary, with thirty men, set out for the sugar camp. When McGary finally reached the maple tree grove, he found the mutilated body of his stepson. While Chief Blackfish failed to take the fort, he did cause the delay of spring preparations for corn planting, so no corn was planted at Harrodsburg during 1777.[155]

Hugh McGary, upset with the death of his stepson, openly expressed his dislike for James Harrod, accusing him of carelessness and cowardice in relationship with the defense of the fort. The dispute grew extremely bitter until the two men leveled their rifles at each other. At this moment, McGary's wife rushed to the scene and pushed her husband's rifle to one side. Harrod then withdrew, and the trouble cooled for the moment.[156]

On March 7, Native Americans appeared around sunrise and set fire to one of the old cabins outside the stockade. The white men, even after the death of Ray, rushed out to extinguish the flames, only to find themselves face to face with an overwhelming number of Indian warriors. Aided by the cover of the forest, the settlers were able to reach the fort. McGary, Joseph Lindsay, John Gass, Jason Ray, Richard Hogan, Ben Linn and others were

Left: A current photo of the grave of Chief Cornstalk at Point Pleasant, West Virginia. *Historical Marker Database.*

Above: A James Harrod Trust Historical Marker for the home of Hugh McGary in Harrodsburg. *Keith Rightmyer.*

in the party and rushed outside to drive them off. When he saw a warrior wearing the shirt his stepson had on when he was killed, McGary became insane with rage, hacked the Indian's body into bits and fed the pieces to his dog. The pioneers brought another dead Native American back to the fort and showed him to the women and children. They then dumped him in a hole and buried him.

The Native Americans killed all the cattle they could find and then left, but small roving bands continued to molest the fort throughout the year. During the above-mentioned attack, several settlers were wounded: Hugh McGary suffered a broken arm and John Gass was slightly wounded in the neck, but both recovered; Archibald McNeal was severely wounded and died twelve days later.[157]

On March 8, several men ventured out from Harrodstown to bring in corn from the corncribs raised the previous year; it took them ten days. George Rogers Clark wrote in his diary, "8 [March 1777] Brought in corn from the different cribs until the 18th day." At nighttime on March 18, Native Americans killed and scalped Hugh Wilson within a half mile of the fort.[158]

Scalping was painful but not always fatal. When scalping someone, an attacker would hold down a victim, grab a handful of hair and cut it at the

A photo of a scalping survivor. *Native Heritage Project.*

base to the bone in a silver dollar–size incision. The attacker would then place a foot on the victim's back for leverage and yank the scalp free. The scalps were then stretched on small wooden hoops and the skin side painted. Scalps were decorated, hung from lodges and cabin lofts and glorified as war trophies. Scalping goes back to antiquity, and its practice was not restricted by race.

For anyone living through scalping, the treatment was almost as bad as being scalped. When "pegging the head," a doctor sat in front of the victim and, with a sharp leather awl, bored numerous holes into the bare skull to allow the pink cranial fluid to ooze through and form a scab. After swabbing with poultices, the head was wrapped and the wound slowly healed, as long as it did not get infected.

There were times when the entire scalp was skinned off. According to an observer during the French and Indian War, "Scalping is the cutting of the skin round the head, and by drawing quite to the eyes." Such a horrendous wound must have been beyond cure.[159]

There are not any accurate inventories of the weapons carried by either the frontier militia or their Indian opponents. The little information we have would indicate that neither side had any standard type of weapon but that white men were frequently armed with rifles, while many of the Native Americans carried smoothbore trade muskets. The rifle had the advantage of being more accurate and killing men at a greater distance. Originally, this advantage was offset by a slow rate of fire. Men trained to use the standard British "Brown Bess" musket could average four shots per minute, but its .75-caliber balls would often miss a man standing only sixty yards away.

A backwoods invention made the rifle more suitable for combat and eventually established its superiority over the musket. Some unknown genius discovered that a greased patch placed over the bullet lessened the time needed to reload and also became a gas check to utilize the full force of the exploding powder. An experienced rifleman using such a patch could fire about three rounds per minute and usually shoot the balls inside an inch target at fifty yards. If anyone wanted to fire faster with a rifle, he could load subsequent rounds using buckshot or an undersized ball. It was discovered in battle that at one hundred yards, only about 40 percent of the musket balls

A historical postcard of a Native American scalping a settler. *Author's collection.*

hit a man-sized target, whereas the rifle accounted for 50 percent accuracy at three hundred yards.

American patch-loading also resulted in economy of ammunition. Because of the increased gas pressure, it was found that a .50-caliber, half-ounce ball was effective, while British smoothbores were made for a .75-caliber one-ounce ball. In other words, shot for shot, the rifle would kill more men at a greater distance using only half the powder and lead. Whenever the

Virginians were protected by a fort, a slow rate of fire was not as important as accuracy. The men on both sides of these walls looked for concealment, and close shots were rare. But out in the open, men could wait until the enemy was near, fire and then charge, expecting to finish the battle with the bayonet or, more often on the frontier, with a knife or tomahawk. Some men found it comforting to carry a pistol into combat, and a few found the combat effectiveness of a double-barrel rifle to be ample compensation for its extra weight.[160]

On March 28, 1777, a large number of Native Americans again attacked Harrodstown. They divided into small parties and waylaid every path and avenue to the fort from the fields or forest, concealing themselves behind trees and bushes. They also attempted to cut off all supplies by killing the cattle. This time, prowling Native Americans, within sight of Fort Harrod, "killed and scalped Garret Pendegrass" (a fort trader) and captured and then killed Peter Flinn; Flinn's body was never found.[161]

On April 3, an alarm was given at daylight, but no fighting took place. On the sixth, Michael Stoner made his way into the fort and reported casualties from Indian attacks as far away as Rye Cove on the Clinch River. On April 9, more warriors were reported in the vicinity of Harrodstown.

In spite of their troubles, on April 19 the defenders at Harrodstown self-consciously continued their civic routines, holding both an election and performing a wedding. The Kentucky settlers elected John Todd and Richard Callaway as the first county representatives to the Virginia legislature. Clark worked without ceasing to improve the military condition of the county.

On Election Day, James Berry married Widow Christina Stagner Wilson (daughter of Barney), whose husband, Hugh Wilson, had been killed on March 7. Hugh and Christina were the parents of the first white child born in Kentucky, Harrod Wilson. The widow had been "in her weeds" just a month and a day—a reference to the archaic term "widow's weeds," a woman's wearing of black clothing to signify mourning for her deceased husband.[162] It should not be thought, however, that her remarriage was evidence of indifference about the loss of her first husband. In this pioneer community, men outnumbered available women more than three to one. Naturally, a widow with small children had a very real need for a husband's protection and support. A man's sympathy for her helpless condition often won reciprocal affection. In any event, early remarriages were common.[163]

Also in April, Clark called on the commanders of the different forts to appoint two patrols, each to alternate searches along the Ohio River, and give notice of Native American approach. These patrols were changed each week. At the same time, Clark dispatched two men to the Illinois country to gather information for a scheme he had in mind.

On April 25, 1777, John Cowan's report of activities stated, "Fresh signs of Indians seen at 2 o'clock. They were heard imitating owls, turkeys, etc. At 4 [o'clock a] sentry spied one and shot at three at 10 o'clock. April 25, Native Americans were lurking around Harrodstown imitating owls, turkeys, and other game, but their decoys were too well understood by the whites to be entrapped by them."

On the morning of April 29, Francis McConnell and James Ray were 100 yards south of the fort shooting at a mark to test their guns. Some Native Americans stole sufficiently near that one of them shot at and mortally wounded McConnell, who fell behind a log. When Ray dashed toward the Indian, thinking there was but one, he was soon attacked by a large body of warriors. He retreated 150 yards to the fort and, finding the gate closed, took refuge behind a stump seven steps from the fort walls, where for about four hours the bullets of the enemy impregnated the earth around him. While this was happening, his mother was a painful spectator from the portholes, but at length Ray exclaimed, "For God's sake, dig a hole under the cabin wall, and take me in!" It was speedily done, and Ray darted through the aperture, safe.

Toward evening, Silas Harlan, James Ray and others opened the fort gate, raised the alarm, ran out and brought in McConnell, who had during the day repeatedly waved his hand for assistance; to favor this sortie, several men got on the cabin roofs and fired in the direction where the Native Americans were hallooing, which, with the yells of Harlan's advancing party, caused the Native Americans to scamper away like partridges. McConnell died shortly after he was brought in and was buried in an unoccupied bastion in the southwest corner of the fort.[164]

By May 1, 1777, the census at Harrodstown was 84 men fit for duty and 4 unfit for duty, 24 women, 12 children over ten, 58 children under ten, 12 slaves over ten and 7 slaves under ten (for a total of 201). There were 22 men at Boonesborough and 15 men at Logan's Station. This made 121 men fit for duty in Kentucky and 40 families, with the total population of Kentucky about 280. Most of the cattle had been killed, and most of the horses stolen. No corn was planted at Harrodstown. Under these grim circumstances, Hugh McGary and John Haggin were sent on May 18 to Fort Pitt to learn the prospects of peace and of recovering the horses stolen by the Native Americans.[165]

At this period, each of the stations furnished two good spies or scouts selected by their captains for the payment of whose services Major Clark pledged the faith of Virginia: Simon Kenton and Thomas Brooks from Boonesborough; Samuel Moore (except when absent on his mission to Illinois) and Bates Collier from Harrodstown; and John Kennedy, John Martin and sometimes John Conrad from Logan's Station. These spies ranged the country as high as the Three Islands above Limestone on the Ohio River and as low as the mouth of the Licking River and were generally able by their skills and vigilance to detect the advent of bands of the enemy and give timely notice of their approach. But when the Native Americans were once again in the country and scattered in squads, sometimes watching a station and then hunting for supplies, the scouts were too few in number always to keep pace with their designs and movements.[166]

With Native Americans still harassing Harrodstown, a party consisting of Squire Boone and several others went out on May 26 in search of the enemy. Passing through some small glades southeast of the fort, the men in advance called out, "Boone, come on!" Squire was lingering behind, examining for fresh moccasin tracks, when he heard some little distance to one side of him the single exclamation "Boone!" Stopping to look, he received a shot in his left side, breaking one of his ribs in two places. The Native Americans, probably few in number, escaped unseen.

Hardly a week went by without one or two deaths because of ordinary activities near the fort or at the home stations. Many deaths were from carelessness. Barney Stagner is one of those legendary deaths. Stagner was a little Dutchman whom James Harrod had made the keeper of the fort springs. Although not an impressive job, it was important, and he took his tasks seriously. The young boys at the fort liked to tease the old man by throwing gourds and rocks into the water just to hear Stagner yell.

Stagner often boasted that the Native Americans would not kill him because he was too old. James Ray heard him make this claim during an Indian attack and told Barney that he should hoist himself up on the fort gate in front of the Native Americans: "Now Barney, you say the Native Americans can't kill you, suppose we hoist you on top of the Fort now and see what the consequences will be."[167]

Barney changed the subject but not his opinion. On June 22, 1777, he carelessly wandered outside the fort above the Big Spring, against Harrod's orders. He was killed and scalped by the Native Americans. They cut off his head and stuck it on a pole. For years after that, the boys living near the fort

A historical postcard of the spring inside the Old Fort Harrod replica. *Author's collection.*

used to say that at night when the moon was full, they could see Barney's ghost around the fort springs.[168]

In June 1777, Detroit lieutenant governor Henry Hamilton began using Native Americans against the settlers in the west. He received an order from the British to employ as many Native Americans as possible in "making a diversion and exciting an arm on the frontiers of Virginia and Pennsylvania." Native Americans were to be properly led to "restrain them from committing violence on the well affected and inoffensive inhabitants." Within a month, Hamilton had sent out fifteen war parties, each of them had on average nineteen warriors and two white men. Six months later, Hamilton had received seventy-two prisoners and 129 scalps, giving him the nickname "Hair Buyer." This policy by the British may have been a serious mistake because it united the frontier as nothing else could have done.[169]

On July 6, a buffalo bull returned to Fort Harrod and was killed for a wedding. The bride was Hannah Soverens, and the wedding took place in Harrodstown. On July 14 and 15, wheat was reaped at Harrodstown. On July 16, Hugh McGary returned from Fort Pitt and reported no prospect of peace or of recovering their stolen horses from the Native Americans.[170]

Benjamin Linn married Hannah Sovereigns, and McGary married several as magistrate. Hannah was sister to John Sovereigns, who with his mother and sister had been captured by the Shawnees, and his

A photo of Detroit lieutenant governor Henry Hamilton greeting his troops.

mother's tongue had been cut by them so she could not talk. They were probably taken before they came to Kentucky. Clark's diary states, "July 9. Lt. Linn married—great merriment." The Sovereigns were from the Monongahela region, and Hannah was about ten when she was captured during the French and Indian War; she was kept for six years. The Sovereigns were among those delivered up at the close of Bonquet's expedition of 1764.[171]

On August 5, a skirmish, soon to be called the "turnip patch incident," occurred. A party of ten or twelve Native Americans had secreted themselves near a turnip patch on the flat north of Fort Harrod, but the alarm shown among the cattle indicated their presence and hiding place. Major Clark with a number of men, including McGary and Ray, crept out of the south gate of the fort, got behind the Native Americans and killed four of them and wounded others; they took plunder that sold for upward of seventy pounds.

On August 11, John Higgins died at Harrodsburg of a lingering disease. His was the first natural death that occurred in Kentucky.[172]

Per historical documents, one day during the summer of 1777, James Harrod was at his cabin busily engaged in cleaning his rifle when a man ran up to him, plainly excited and breathing heavily. The man said, "Jim Bailey's cabin has been attacked by the red men and no one is alive to tell the tale, save his two daughters, who have been carried away by the savages in the direction of their village. Unless a party hurries immediately in pursuit, they will be taken to the tribe and will never be seen again. Their fate will not be a pleasant one."

Harrod jumped to his feet immediately, saying that he would go at once; the man was to run and tell the other settlers to send help. Grabbing his powder horn and pouch of bullets, he headed out, bursting through the tangled woodland. Arriving at the cabin, he saw that a terrible fight had occurred around the little log fortress. Smoke was still coming from the chimney, the windows were broken and the door was a splintered wreck. The tracks of the Native Americans were plain because a rain had fallen, and it was evident that eight or ten had been in the party.

It was near midday when Harrod turned to follow the trail of the Native Americans. After an hour's travel, it became evident that the Native Americans had separated. One half had gone toward the Indian towns, and the other half had sheared off toward a settlement, about fifteen miles below. Presuming that the Native Americans would take the girls to the settlement by the nearest route, he followed the first trail. As night came on, he was delighted to see a campfire before him in the dense woodland.

A true woodsman, Harrod dropped to his knees and cautiously moved toward the glimmering embers. From behind a fallen log, he saw five Native Americans lying near the blaze. The two captive girls were bound with deer thongs, and he could see the misery on their pale faces.

Creeping to a large oak tree, he saw one Indian who seemed to be keeping guard over the others, but even he was sleepy. Finally, the guard seated himself and then rested on the ground by the side of his companions. Harrod saw his opportunity and began to crawl toward the camp.

According to a historian, Harrod "[drew] his tomahawk and [brained] two of the sleeping Native Americans, [which] was but the work of a moment, and, as he was about to strike the third one, the handle turned in his fingers, and the savage received the blow on the side instead of the center of his head. He awoke with a yell. It was his last. Grasping his weapon more firmly, the frontiersman struck the fellow with a surer blow and dropped him lifeless to the ground. With a terrific whoop he now sprang for his rifle just as the two other Native Americans rose to escape, and, firing hastily, one of them fell to rise no more."

The other man ran into the forest, but Harrod stopped, taking careful aim; he threw his tomahawk at his enemy. It lopped off one of the Indian's ears and cut a deep gash in his cheek, but he kept running. Harrod found the two captive girls crying bitterly. He untied them and embraced them both.

Back at the fort, the two girls were carried on the men's shoulders into camp, and they were given a feast of welcome. Harrod's modesty kept him away from the ceremony. The next day, he left on a hunting excursion. He was not seen until a week later, when he returned with several deer and bear skins.[173]

On September 11, a party of thirty-seven men under Colonel Bowman went to Captain Joseph Bowman's settlement at the Cove Spring, five miles southeast of Harrodstown, to shell corn and bring back to the fort. The "corncrib skirmish" occurred on September 22 when a party of Kickapoos stole up through a canebrake and fired on the white men as they were shelling corn. Bowman gallantly hallooed to his men, "Stand your ground!—we are able to beat them, by the Lord!" Squire Boone and six others were injured (one later died that night). Eli Gerrard was killed. This spirited little affair was also known among the frontiersmen of the day as the Battle of Cove Spring.[174]

Corn had been raised at the Cove Spring near Harrod's run and some five miles southeast of Harrodstown. A few days later, another party went there to shell corn in the cribs, and Native Americans came upon them. James Berry was very severely wounded, and two were killed and another wounded who subsequently died. The men fought. Nathaniel Randolph ran all the way to Harrodsburg, got help and returned; the men were still on the offensive, and the Native Americans were moving off.[175]

A historical postcard of an agricultural scene during the pioneer days of Kentucky. *Author's collection.*

An early log-construction corncrib and shed at the Oconaluftee Mountain Farm Museum, Cherokee, North Carolina. *Galen Parks Smith.*

The Kickapoos were Algonquins from Illinois and Wisconsin whose nomadic travels took them as far as Texas and Mexico. The Kickapoos shared many cultural and linguistic traits with the Shawnees, causing many anthropologists to speculate that these two tribes were once more closely related. According to Kickapoo oral tradition itself, the Shawnees and the Kickapoos were indeed one people once, but an argument over a bear's foot caused a split. French Jesuits were the first to mention the group. During the era of colonialism and conquest, much of the Kickapoo nation was absorbed by the culturally similar Mascoutens (Foxes), who in turn, after the French Beaver Wars of 1720s, sought protection through alliance with the Sauks.[176]

During the fall of 1777, George Rogers Clark returned to Virginia with an ambitious plan to push the British out of the Ohio Valley region. Governor Patrick Henry approved the scheme, commissioned Clark as a lieutenant colonel and authorized him to raise seven militia companies of fifty men each. Governor Henry wanted the troops mustered west of the Blue Ridge, but fewer men than expected responded to the call. Clark and his volunteers made their plans to return to Kentucky.[177]

A photo titled "Kickapoo: Babe Shkit, Chief and Delegate from Oklahoma." Originally created for the Smithsonian Institution Bureau of American Ethnology.

Harrod never suffered any injuries during the numerous Native American attacks, but he did end up with two broken bones related to hunting trips, both incidents happening in the same way. Harrod liked to do his hunting on horseback because he needed the extra speed for chasing down buffalo, deer and elk, but managing a long rifle while mounted was risky to say the least.

Both of Harrod's accidents happened when he fired and his horse reared up and threw him off; he broke his thigh bones.[178]

While Harrod did fight Native Americans, he did so only when he had to. Some of his friends killed because they wanted the scalps, but Harrod did not. Once when he was on a hunting trip, some Native Americans chased him over a river, and he hid behind a tree. As three Native Americans crossed the river, he fired, killing one and wounding one; the third got away. Later, Harrod went back to the area and found the wounded man. He spoke to the man and took care of his wound; then he took him to a cave where he fed and cared for him. When the Native American man was able to walk again, Harrod sent him back to his tribe. Years later, when Daniel Boone was captured, he said it was the same native Harrod saved.[179]

James Harrod tried to keep things running cheerfully and smoothly, but it was no fun to be cooped up in the fort all summer. Nerves were frayed, and women were quarreling and gossiping. One visitor from Virginia during that summer complained that the women were constantly pestering him with their questions about the happenings back home. He said they were dirty and their children scruffy.

This arrogant visitor didn't stay long enough to learn the reason for the disorder at the fort. He didn't know that the women were starved for news from their old homes and had very little to occupy their thoughts during the summer-long Native American siege. He didn't know the emotional effect of daily killings and the danger and sorrow at every cabin door. He didn't know the threat of going down to the washtub spring outside the fort walls to scrub dirt out of greasy clothes with bare hands scuffing against the stones, all the while terrified that a bullet or an arrow would come out of nowhere. The women were never safe outside the fort during the summer of 1777, but they could only stand the dirty, smelly clothes so long before venturing into danger to clean them. By the autumn of 1777, most of the settlers in Kentucky were living in Fort Harrod, Fort Boonesborough or Logan's Station.[180]

A skillful hunter, James Harrod was always generous with his spoils; a brave man by nature, he always led his men, taking the greatest risks himself. If a family were in want, Harrod went to their assistance; if settlers were attacked by Native Americans, Harrod went to their rescue; if a horse was lost, Harrod trailed it and returned it to its owner. He went on not only exploring expeditions but also expeditions against the Native Americans. No labor was too great and no enterprise too hazardous for him to undertake. Primarily, he was a woodsman; his bold, free nature loved the open land, and he seemed happiest when wandering through the forest, hunting and trapping.[181]

Colonel John Bowman was the newly appointed county lieutenant for the new Kentucky militia, and he arrived with a large company of volunteer militia to protect the territory. Unfortunately, most of the men had only enlisted for a short time. Harrod was able to persuade many of these men to lengthen their stay to help protect Kentucky. Assisted by Harrod, Boone and Logan, Bowman jumped into his job of coordinating defenses for all three forts.[182]

On September 2, 1777, the first court was held in Harrodsburg, Kentucky. The elected judges were John Bowman, Richard Callaway, John Floyd, John Todd and Benjamin Logan. John May was the official surveyor, and Levi Todd was the court clerk. Levi Todd was the grandfather of Mary Todd Lincoln, wife of President Abraham Lincoln. Also, during this time, Harrod became a justice in Kentucky County.[183]

In December 1777, Colonel Bowman sent a letter addressed to General Edward Hand, then appointed by George Washington as a brigadier general in command at Pittsburgh, furnishing some hints about the condition of Kentucky County at this time:

Harrodsburg, December 12, 1777

Sir,

We received yours by Mr. John Haggin, dated Fort Randolph, 18th November 1777, which news gives great satisfaction to the poor Kentucky people, who have these twelve months past been confined to three forts, on which the Native Americans have made several fruitless attempts. They are left almost without horses sufficient to supply the stations, as we are obliged to get all our provisions out of the woods. The Native Americans have burned all our corn they could find the past summer, as it was in cribs at different plantations some distance from the garrisons, and no horses on which to bring it in. At this time, we have no more than two months bread—near 200 women and children and not able to send them to the inhabitants; many of those families left desolate widows with small children destitute of necessary clothing. Necessity has obliged many of our young men to go to the Mo-non-ga-hale, their former place of abode, for clothing, intending to join their respective companies as soon as possible, and as there will be a sufficient guard. I think it proper to order some

corn from this place for our support. We intend to keep possession of the country, and plant crops in the ensuring spring, as we have no other place from which to expect relief. If we are denied this request, we must do without bread till we can get it from what we intend to plant. I find it difficult to keep the garrisons plenty in meat, and if we have no bread, we must at any rate suffer.

Your humb. serv't,

John Bowman
Flavored by Lieut. Linn[184]

During the autumn, many young men returned east to their old homes to provide themselves with a new supply of clothing. Those who remained necessarily had to rely on the skins of wild beasts for clothing, together with the homely product of the wild nettle and buffalo. The wild prickly nettle is a plant of luxurious growth in the west, attaining a height of three to four feet, with a bark of fiber somewhat resembling that of flax and hemp or rather of a character between the two. The stalk falls when touched with frost, and when the fiber matures or rots by the rains or snows, it is separated from the stalk and spun. A coarse article of cloth was manufactured from it, and sometimes it was combined with the coarse wool or hair from the

An unusual double postcard of the replica of Old Fort Harrod when the park was still called Pioneer Memorial Park. *Author's collection.*

buffalo, the nettle being used as warp and the buffalo wool as filling. For the manufacture of socks, buffalo wool alone was used, which was quite soft and wore very well.[185]

Not only were the Native American attacks the most frequent and violent during this year, but the winter of 1777–78 was the worst ever endured by the pioneers. The temperature dropped to twenty degrees below zero. The rivers and springs froze solid, and travel was impossible. The bears, buffalo and smaller wildlife were often found starved and frozen to death. There was no food or water, and Indian attacks came almost daily. Many pioneer men, women and children died of starvation and dehydration. The other pioneers were able to survive, but they lost all of their livestock and many friends.

The fort held. Fort Harrod was the only Kentucky fort that was never breached.

Chapter 7

1778

James Harrod Takes a Wife

*Family life was important to recent immigrants and backcountry settlers, and
James Harrod…eventually married Ann Coburn McDaniel in 1778.*
—*Andrew K. Frank,* Early Republic: People and Perspectives

The hostilities were not all because of war-hungry tribesmen. Harrod learned from his brother, William, that the powerful Shawnee chief Cornstalk, who in 1777 was held hostage at Fort Randolph at the mouth of the Great Kanawha, was attacked and killed by a party of irresponsible backwoodsmen. James Harrod knew that this would destroy any peace left in the Ohio Valley. This immediately caused William to abandon Grove Creek Fort in Moundville and take his men to Fort Wheeling, while the settlers planned to go on to Fort Pitt. However, William received a leg wound from a Native American's bullet and ended up returning to Tenmile to heal.

Up until now, James Harrod had no interest in starting a family. Early in his career, he had been too busy, and many times too far from the settlement, to find a woman and marry. But now Kentucky was growing, and he thought it would be nice to have a household and a wife to make it cozy. In early 1778, in his mid-thirties, he took a shine to twenty-two-year-old widow Ann Coburn McDaniel. Ann made a good match for James because he was one of the finest men in Kentucky. He was strong, energetic, smart and gentle mannered, and he had the best pieces of land in the country.[186]

An illustration of Shawnee chief Cornstalk about to be murdered from a 1920 children's book by Ada Budell.

Ann was small, beautiful and educated—seemingly too cultured to fit into the rough environment in which she had to live. She had come to Kentucky in 1776 with her first husband, James McDaniel, who was killed by Native Americans the same year at Drennon's Lick. In late 1777, Ann's father, with whom she lived at Logan's Station, was also killed and scalped by Native Americans while picking corn between Logan's and Harrod's forts. She had a two-year-old son, James McDaniel Jr., whom James Harrod would come to love as his own.

In mid-February 1778, the Harrod wedding took place at Logan's Station. February was a quiet time at the fort because Native American tribesmen were in their camps, waiting for spring, and this gave settlers time for a big celebration. New supplies of jerked meat were stowed away, and the ground was too frozen to prepare for the new crops, so it was time for a party. Robert Todd, one of the magistrates of Kentucky County, officiated on the occasion.

Harrod's wedding was probably typical for frontier affairs, with the groom arriving at noon and the celebration lasting until the next day. By today's standards, it was probably a boring affair, with no silver, fine china or pure Irish linen to cover the table and no beautiful flowers or soft music, just

A photo of the current buildings at Logan's Station in Stanford, Kentucky. *Keith Rightmyer.*

the seesaw of a screaming violin accompanied by tapping feet and clapping hands, keeping time to "The Mouse Trap":[187]

> *Of all the simple things we do,*
> *To rub o-ver a whim-si-cal life,*
> *There's no one fol-ly is so true*
> *As that ve-ry bar-gain a wife.*
> *We're just like a mouse in a trap*
> *Or rat that is caught in a gin;*
> *We start and fret, and try to escape,*
> *And rue the sad hour we came in.*[188]

Ann had one ruffled dress and a brooch she brought across the mountains. Jim wore a new hunting shirt and leggings. It is believed that Thomas was the only Harrod sibling to attend the wedding, but Sam could also have been there. Will Harrod was busy in Monongahela country helping outfit Clark's Illinois regiment.

Because it was such a long trip to Williamsburg to get a marriage license, James and Ann married without one. This would bother Ann in later years when she was involved in lawsuits over her inheritance. In later years, she took great pains to prove the legality of her wedding.

The ceremony preceded a dinner of all the best the pioneers had to offer. The warm weather of this particular February had started a new flow of maple sap, so the couple had hasty pudding, a favorite dessert made with cornmeal mush and baked with molasses. Bear meat and venison with kraut were also favorite dishes. Gourds and wooden plates held food, and there may have been a few pewter cups to hold milk or toddy.[189]

A dried apple stack cake was a form of pioneer wedding cake that may have been served. Because wedding cakes were so expensive, neighbors brought cake layers to donate to the bride's family. The dough would be rolled or pressed out into very thin layers and baked in cast-iron skillets. The family of the bride cooked, sweetened and spiced dried apples to spread between the layers of the cake. The number of layers in the wedding cake was a gauge of the bride's popularity. The average cake had seven to eight layers, but sometimes there would be twelve. The dried apple stack cake

A photo of a dried apple stack cake similar to ones made during the pioneer days. *Matt Hulsman.*

recipe was supposedly brought to Kentucky by James Harrod along the Wilderness Trail.[190]

After dinner, the fun really began as the dancing started, with the bride and groom jigging off the first reel. Jokes and games were abundant, and everyone had fun until the girls pulled the bride to one side and led her up to the cabin loft. When she was tucked securely into bed, the men carried the groom up the ladder and dropped him on the cornhusk mattress beside his bride.

Dancing continued in the room below, with the occasional intermission to take drinks to the newlyweds. Closer to morning, the women placed a huge bowl of kraut or hominy before the couple, and the newlyweds had to eat it all before the guests below would leave them alone. By midmorning, the last guest was gone, and the couple went to their own home, where another crowd would give them a rousing welcome.[191]

Harrod's new station at Boiling Spring was incomplete and too isolated for safety, so he took Ann straight on to Fort Harrod, where they lived until the next fall. Boiling Spring became Harrod's Station. Although no exact description exists, it is said to have been several cabins surrounded by a stockade. Living there were the Henry Prathers; the Isaac Pritchards; Samuel and Margaret Coburn (Ann Harrod's parents) and her brother's family, the James Coburns; Jacob Kelly; and several of Harrod's nephews. Harrod's Station was fortified in 1779.

Ann had a foreboding idea that her bad luck had not run out. Many people noted that she was superstitious, although later she denied this. Frontiersmen thought that dreams had special significance. Ann told an early Kentucky historian about one particular dream: "I dreamed one night that the Native Americans attacked some of our men outside the fort; and that my husband ran out to help them. I saw an Indian shoot him, and, when he fell, stoop over and stab him. The very next day, three men were chopping upon a log on the creek along the side of old Harrod's fort, close by, when we heard guns fire and saw the three men killed and the Native Americans scalping them."[192]

Regardless of her dreams, Ann scarcely had time to grieve the death of her father because she was too busy, helping James to greet the many new settlers arriving to Harrodstown during the summer of 1778. She had to teach the women to make linsey and show them where to find the best herbs for the "itch" and what to do for snakebites and fever. Ann Harrod spoke about women and guns, saying, "I never could do much with a gun. I have tried it often, but never could succeed. I did manage to kill a [buffalo] cow and a bear, or the girls would never have got done laughing at me."[193]

An illustrated map of Corn Island near the Falls of the Ohio. *Wikimedia Commons.*

On May 27, 1778, George Rogers Clark arrived back at the falls of the Ohio, and his men began planting corn and felling trees to establish a small outpost on Corn Island. The recently mustered militia would rendezvous here for Clark's push into Illinois on June 24. The day the militia pulled out, there was a solar eclipse, causing misconceptions of superstitions among the men.[194]

Lieutenant James Trabue was appointed to serve as purchasing commissary to provide provisions to Kentucky's current forts: Boonesborough, Harrodstown, Logan's and Louisville. One of the hardest tasks was keeping the gunpowder in the magazines dry. When the kegs of powder get damp, the mix of saltpeter, ash and sulfur would separate, with the saltpeter settling to the bottom and the ash and sulfur lumping on the top. The kegs had to be upended and rotated or opened and the powder dried and shifted.[195]

Harrod and his new wife lived at Fort Harrod until he could fortify Boiling Spring and build Ann a large twin-chimney frame house. This was the first house of its kind in Kentucky; unfortunately, it was destroyed by arson in 1833. At this site alone, Harrod had a total of 2,818 acres in what is now Mercer and Boyle Counties. He had numerous other landholdings in Kentucky, particularly along the Green River south of his settlement. Because of the spaciousness of their home, the hospitality of Ann and the somewhat safe location, their house became a preaching place and stopover for early Methodist itinerant preachers.

Around 1778, Job Chapman and John Stapleton left Harrodstown in the summer, some 150 yards south from Harrod's Station at Boiling Spring, in the field to get a piggin of beans. Native Americans were concealed in the corn field, and Chapman was shot dead, a ball passing through the piggin (a small wooden pail with one stave extended upward as a handle) and into his body; Stapleton had his arm broken and escaped to Fort Harrod. He seized his gun and tried to run out to pursue the Native Americans with his broken arm. A party went out, but the Native Americans had gone; Chapman was found scalped, a spear sticking in his breast.[196]

Boiling Spring continued to grow and flourish, and the fortification was never successfully breached by Native American attacks. Many families are known to have lived within the station and on Harrod's land, including the Coburns, Kellys, Prathers, Pritchards and two of Harrod's nephews. The Harrod's Station also housed an influx of the Low Dutch, whom Harrod allowed to build cabins and clear and farm land until they could fortify their own claims. The Old Dutch Station was established nearby on the outskirts of Harrod's land.

Big game was pushing west, and salt was getting extremely hard to acquire. Salt making was one of the most tedious jobs a man could do. It was also dangerous because the Native Americans, when in a scalp-collecting mood, would watch the salt licks. The company had to post guards day and night.[197]

The saline content of the springs was usually too low to make salt quickly. At large licks, there would be three or four furnaces going all the time, but it took eight hundred to one thousand gallons of the brackish water to produce a bushel of salt. Kettles used for salt making typically had a twenty- to thirty-gallon capacity. The pioneers had a saying that a lazy man was not worth his salt; in fact, it took a cow and a calf to balance the scales for a bushel of the vital commodity.[198]

Harrod talked with the men of Fort Harrod, and sixteen men decided to go with him to buy or make salt. They headed out in the middle of October 1778 to the falls of Ohio. As a boy, he had visited a large spring about three miles west of Kaskaskia across the Mississippi River. In Ohio, they bought a keelboat, which was a light boat, sharp at both ends, sixty to eighty feet long and eight to ten feet wide. It was fitted with a cabin, removable mast and sails and running boards along the sides where men could stand as they poled upstream.

Once during this time, Harrod tied up at the bank and went ashore to check his directions with a few Delawares and their wives who were camping near the shore. The Native Americans were reluctant to talk until Harrod produced a bottle of rum. Once the Delawares were drunk, they agreed that one of them would go with their "white brother" as guide and protector. The guide staggered to the boat and promptly fell asleep. When he woke, they were fifty to sixty miles downstream. They quickly learned that the Delaware brave would be no help, so they sent him ashore and told him they had only gone about five miles.

At the salt works, Harrod's group found men with furnaces blazing and water boiling in leaden and iron kettles. Harrod bought all the salt they had, paying for it in Continental money instead of bartering because the men were not inclined to take goods in exchange for so valuable a commodity.

On the return trip, they met two Frenchmen paddling from Vincennes. They told Harrod that more than four hundred Cherokees were waiting at the mouth of the Cumberland River to kill the Kentuckians. A little farther on, they met another Frenchman who confirmed the story. The small group left the river and continued on to Harrodstown on foot.

The success of the salt trip was not the last of Harrod's "lucky streak." At Christmastime, he heard good news from Virginia. Judge Henderson had presented a memorial to the House of Representatives asking for a validation of the title of his claims, but the House refused the request, stating "that all purchases of lands made or to be made, within the chartered bounds of the Commonwealth, as described by the constitution or form of government, by any private persons not authorized by public authority, are void."[199]

They decided because of the great expense of making purchases and settling lands that it was "just and reasonable" to allow Richard Henderson and company compensation for trouble and expense. The Senate voted to allot them land on Green River, land far inferior to the original claim.[200]

This was a great victory for Harrod. While the creation of Kentucky County two years earlier had voided the Transylvania claim, now it had been voided by Virginia law. At last, the promise Harrod had made to his party of thirty-one men back in 1774 would hold good—they could claim their land under old Virginia law. James was now a man with titled property surrounded by friends and kinfolk.

Chapter 8

1779–1780

THE HARD WINTER AND BEYOND

The inhabitant's avered they never knew so severe weather at that season.
—Newton D. Mereness, "Journal of Colonel William Fleming,"
Mereness's Travels in the American Colonies

The Kentucky settlers marked the Hard Winter of 1779–80 as the hardest they ever endured. The Ohio and Cumberland Rivers froze, stopping the flow of supplies to the settlers. Heavy snow that fell in October did not melt in some areas until March. Weeks of below-freezing temperatures wiped out livestock and wildlife, creating starving times for folks west of the Blue Ridge; many people froze to death or died from exposure or sickness.[201]

During the winter of 1779, Harrod received a permanent military commission as a colonel, and the same year he was elected to be Kentucky County's representative to the Virginia legislature along with Colonel Richard Calloway. Harrod's main contribution to the legislature was a bill for improvement of the Wilderness Road, which the assembly passed in October.[202]

The population had exploded since George Rogers Clark's campaign, so Harrod had little time for concern over militia rank or legislative duties. With passage of the new land laws, prospective settlers were organizing east of Harrodsburg, and Pennsylvanians were also sailing down the Ohio. One farmer said that the new settlers bound for Kentucky were as thick as butterflies in July. The reason for the rush was because hearings on land claims were to begin in October with the arrival of four commissioners from Virginia, and everyone wanted their rights established by then.[203]

Harrod liked the new law because it allowed two rights, settlement and preemption. For anyone who had been in the country before January 1, 1778, and had raised a crop of corn on any unclaimed land, they were entitled to four hundred acres. Those who established themselves, as most of Harrod's men had, could obtain as much as one thousand adjoining acres at a rate of forty-three pounds per one hundred acres in Virginia money, equivalent to ten shillings per one hundred acres in colonial money.[204]

There was a catch in the law, even for Harrod's men. Virginia had made no provision for supervising the surveys, an omission that led to more heartbreak over a long period of years than any amount of Native American trouble. After all, when someone put in a claim to a piece of his land, Harrod could not duel with him nor could he settle the controversy through arguments, for it was necessary to bring witnesses. Most legal trouble came later.[205]

With land prices increasing, Harrod sold one in-lot and three out-lots in Harrodstown with five hundred adjoining acres for three hundred pounds.[206] The men who were sent to settle original land claims were familiar to Harrod and were headed by Colonel William Fleming, from the Point Pleasant campaign. The commissioners had little to guide them since the land law required settlers furnish the direct location of their cabins as precisely as possible so others would be able to determine the boundaries with certainty.[207]

The commissioners used well-known spots as the basis for determination of boundaries: Harrod's Landing, Fort Harrod, Chaplin's Fork, Harrod's Creek and so on. Harrod testified frequently during this session of land court, especially for members of his family. For his stepson, "James Harrod this day appeared and claimed a right to a settlement and preemption as guardian to James McDaniel." This was referring to land on Gilbert's Creek, settled in 1776 by the boy's late father: "The Courts are of the opinion the McDonald heir at law to the decedent has a right to a settlement of four hundred acres of land including the improvement and a preemption of one thousand acres of land adjoining and that a certificate should be issued for it." Harrod also testified for his wife in her claim of 1,400 acres in Ohio, fifty miles below the falls. On his own behalf, Harrod claimed settlement and preemption to a tract of land lying on Harrod's Run now known as Boiling Spring because of the improvements made in 1774, 1775 and 1776.[208]

A photo of the James Harrod Blockhouse at Old Fort Harrod. This was used as Kentucky's land office in the 1780s. *Keith Rightmyer.*

The land office opened in 1779 and was located at Harrodstown. Outlying lands as well as town lots were given consideration for settlements and improvements. Just as soon as it was safe to dwell outside of the stockade, lots were improved with log dwellings.[209]

Severe snow and cold from November 1779 until the middle of March 1780 had harsh effects on the settlers. Deer coats grew thick, the buffalo turned weak very early and geese flew over cabins and forts in long Vs. The Ohio River froze over, and the Kentucky River had ice two feet thick. Cattle died and wolves, beavers and otters froze to death in the woods; streams froze and fish died. Cane offered protection and winter fodder for buffalo, but when the canebrakes sleeted over, buffalo couldn't eat the tall grass and they starved. Turkeys froze to death roosting in trees with their nose slits frozen over. "The hogs were frozen to death, the deer, not able to get water or food, were found dead in great numbers."[210]

Maple trees cracked as their sap froze until they burst open. Water was so scarce that a single Johnny cake would be divided into a dozen portions and distributed to families to make two meals. This finally failed, and the settlers survived on emaciated wild game; some people ate cows and horses that perished in the lots. Many settlers roasted buffalo skins to eat, and others died for want of provisions and lack of solid food.[211]

Nearly everyone was sick, many settlers developed frostbite and some died from the cold. Harrod, normally a very healthy man, developed rheumatism caused by wearing porous deerskin moccasins and leggings. Colonel Fleming noted that the number of illnesses, especially fever and dysentery, in Harrodstown was because the spring below the fort was washing down putrefied flesh, dead dogs, horse, cow and hog excrements, along with the ashes and sweepings of filthy cabins. He noted that the pioneers steeped skins and washed "every sort of dirty rags and clothes in the spring," poisoning the water and making it "the most filthy, nauseous potation imaginable."[212]

Spring brought relief as some fruit trees thrived and vegetable patches flourished, but it also brought new worries. Native Americans fired on grain boats as they floated down the Ohio. The Cherokees were causing problems for the settlers on the Cumberland Trace, so Harrod gathered a company from his fort and Logan's to stop the raids on the new settlers. Most of the trouble in the south came from Cherokee chief Moon. Harrod and his men hid near the Warrior's Path to ambush Moon and his followers. Harrod killed Chief Moon with the first shot, and the other Cherokees fled. In victory, Harrod returned to Harrodstown with Moon's scalp and an ornament made of a silver plate attached to a belt that the chief had worn. This trophy stayed in the Harrod family for many years but was eventually lost by his grandchildren.[213]

During the spring of 1780, James Harrod's brother Samuel was killed by Native Americans on a return trip from New Orleans to trade skins for gunpowder. The attack happened at the mouth of the Tennessee River, and it is believed that the Native American who killed Samuel had been hired by Frenchmen who were angry with William Harrod for arresting their countrymen. James Harrod always said that he owed his success to the patience and interest paid to him by his brother Sam. Samuel had acted both as brother and father to James and William by teaching them to hunt and trap, work with wood and deal with Native Americans.[214]

During this time, the British were planning an offensive march into the west. The English were hoping to drive down from the Mackinac River and attack into Kentucky in hopes of diverting Virginians' attention from the upper Mississippi posts. Clark was planning his 1780 campaign into Ohio to prevent this attack.

Harrod and the first settlers had suffered through the fall of several forts, which, unfortunately, became commonplace. In hindsight, the settlers realized that they should have chosen fewer remote locations and united their power in order to defeat the Native Americans. When the British and Indian allies captured Ruddle's and Martin's stations on the Licking River, Harrod and

A state highway marker for Ruddle's Station. *Dave Knoch.*

his men realized that a new element seemed to be threatening all of Kentucky. The settlers knew that the British had artillery cannons but had never seen them used. Suddenly, the British launched an attack near the Licking River, and Kentuckians were in shock.[215]

Early in the summer of 1780, the commander at Detroit dispatched British captain Henry Bird with a militia of 150 white men and 100 Native Americans to take the falls of the Ohio, or present-day Louisville. On their march down the Miami River, Bird's men recruited more allied Native Americans to aid in their fight, bringing his total to 850 men. On June 22, Bird's campaigns silently surrounded and attacked the patriot settlement of Ruddle's Station, Kentucky. After only a few shots from Bird's artillery, the fort surrendered, and then the unthinkable happened.[216]

While Captain Bird and his men were inside working out the terms of surrender—the settlers would be taken alive and kept as prisoners of war—the Native Americans rushed through the gates and killed 20 of the 350 settlers. Then they grabbed men, women or children and proceeded to strip the people and their cabins of every possession. Soon the Native Americans were beyond Captain Bird's control. From there, the invaders rushed to Martin's Station, five miles away, and captured it in the same way. Bird wanted to protect the prisoners of war, but all the Native Americans wanted to do was divide the spoils of war. Marching on with the prisoners would prove hard because of Native American mistreatment and lack of food. Captain Bird realized that he would have to return the prisoners to Detroit before he could continue on. On the way to Detroit, the Native Americans massacred more than half of the prisoners. On August 4, Captain Bird reached Detroit with only 150 prisoners; these prisoners were held for the remainder of the war.[217]

It was hard for Captain Bird to keep the Native Americans from attacking Lexington's and Bryan's Stations instead of returning to Detroit. Harrod and Clark couldn't understand why Bird decided to stop at this point since the whole expedition was supposed to hand out a deathblow to Kentucky's defenses in the north.[218]

There were several possibilities for Captain Bird's decision. The water of the Licking was low and could endanger the rolling artillery. This was probably the biggest reason since the artillery was extremely heavy and

A photo of the Martin's Station replica. *Historic Martin's Station.*

slow moving. There was the real possibility of starvation, especially for the prisoners, as the Native Americans had slaughtered all the settlers' cattle and destroyed crops. Another explanation was that the British commander was too humane to allow his out-of-control army of revenge-seeking Native Americans to go farther, but this has not been historically proven.[219]

For weeks after this tragedy, rumors filtered into Harrodstown, and Harrod's settlers lived in daily terror. They knew that their stout stockade would not survive the impact of the British cannonballs. Abraham Chaplin, who had been captured by Native Americans and taken to Detroit the year before, had managed to escape and return to Harrodstown with shocking news. He reported that the British were alarmed by the substantial number of settlers arriving in Kentucky and were determined to dislodge them from the west once and for all.[220]

In 1780, when Martin's and Ruddell's Stations were taken, the spies of Harrodstown were on the lookout. When the Native Americans advanced on other forts, the Kentucky County militia prevented the enemy advancements on the rocky banks of the Kentucky River. Ruddell and others from the captured forts went on to live at Logan's Station, and some went to Fort Harrod.[221]

A steady supply of new recruits served to ease Kentuckians' fears, but as summer passed with no more news of the British expedition, the people almost forgot that they were in serious danger. Land speculators swarmed the surveyor's office at Fort Harrod, flashing Virginia treasury warrants and preemption warrants in the faces of early settlers who lacked the means or knowledge to prove the prior rights and consequently looked on this kind of threat as more real and pressing than possible Indian attacks.[222]

The speculators would gather on Harrod's front porch or at the big table in his main living room to draw plat maps of their new surveys, unaware of the indignation they were causing among Harrod's old followers. Always hospitable to visitors, James welcomed them, but he knew that his friends disapproved of him hosting the speculators.[223]

Harrod became alarmed by Virginia's indifference to Kentucky's uncertain political status and by the British/Native American dangers threatening the area. He called together the older settlers and drew up a petition to the Continental Congress:

> *We are situate* [sic] *from six hundred to one thousand miles from our present set of government. Whereby criminals are suffered to escape with impunity, great numbers who was occasionally absent and deprived of an opportunity of their just right improvements…while at the same time they were unable to determine whether the country out of right out to belong to the United States or the state of Virginia. They have by another late act required of us to swear allegiance to the state of Virginia in particular notwithstanding we have already taken the oath of allegiance to the United States. After dilating on the accumulated grievances, the pioneers asked that the Continental Congress take proper methods to form us into a separate state or grant such rules and regulations as they think proper.*[224]

Signing this petition were 640 settlers, including Harrod, his nephew and a combination of early settlers and new arrivals. Many of the signers were from Monongahela country, where anger with Virginia was strong because of the Virginia-Pennsylvania "Westsylvania" border crisis. Monongahelan influence was rising, with three hundred boats and three thousand or more immigrants coming down the Ohio River that year.

Harrod's position on the land dispute was precarious. The Transylvania Company was interested in buying up as much land as possible, so they often had disagreements with individuals over land interests. Now, wealthy Virginian speculators had arrived with treasury warrants to buy up all the unused land, so a complicated struggle started between people with opposing claims. Then there were the Monongahelan and Pennsylvanian settlers who disputed Virginia's right to grant land and who were looking to the national government for support. Finally, there were men like Harrod, who settled in Kentucky without financial backing, basing their hopes on old Virginia settlement law and the Treaty of Fort Stanwix.[225]

Harrod wanted to be friends with all of these disparate parties, and being one of the largest landowners in Kentucky, he saw eye to eye with the large speculators but was not the kind of man to desert old friends who supported his earlier efforts. He also could not speak out against the extremists from Western Pennsylvania. Harrod had no understanding or interest in the legal or political implications. Kentucky needed more people and law and order; numbers meant security and prosperity.

Virginia was doing little to change the situation. Even the old settlers were complaining. The division of the area into three counties (Lincoln, Jefferson and Lafayette) with the establishment of Kentucky district did not appease them.

A state highway marker for Fort Jefferson. *Historical Marker Database.*

They complained about the people pouring into Kentucky. They even complained about George Rogers Clark because of his new Fort Jefferson at the mouth of the Ohio.[226]

Five miles below the mouth of the Ohio River, they were having trouble understanding the addition of a new fort when they were already experiencing difficulty supplying the older establishments. They should not have worried because within short order, Clark, plagued with Native American attacks and supply difficulties, abandoned Fort Jefferson.[227]

When Clark learned of the attacks on Ruddle and Martin stations, he went straight to Harrodstown to plan with Harrod and the militia for a counterattack against the Ohio country and Detroit. When he arrived, he expressed amusement to Harrod over the people's indifference to the danger threatening Kentucky. They were talking of nothing but land and buzzing around the land office. Clark first ordered a detachment to Crab Orchard at the foot of the Cumberland to stop and disarm any who might return to Virginia. He then went into the land office and told the surveyor that he, Clark, would take the entire blame and responsibility for the action. He closed the place, posting a notice that it would not be reopened until after the expedition against the Native Americans.[228]

Among the first names on Clark's list was Simon Kenton, a man who knew personally how Native Americans can be because he had escaped to Harrodstown after months of captivity among the Shawnees. The Native Americans at first thought they had caught Harrod. Eager to retaliate against Harrod for bringing so many white men into the Native American hunting grounds, they beat Kenton and made him ride through the forest naked and strapped on the back of a horse, among other tortures, until

In Memory of
SIMON KENTON
(1755-1836)

who is buried here. During the Revolutionary War he frequently served as scout under George Rogers Clark, and later praised Clark for his role in saving the Kentucky settlements. Kenton's Indian captivity of 1778-79 acquainted him with the Mad River Country where he subsequently provided leadership in its development. Though a legendary frontier scout and rifleman, Kenton was never biased against the Indians.

THE OHIO GUN COLLECTORS ASSOCIATION
AND
1987   THE OHIO HISTORICAL SOCIETY   3-11

A state highway marker for Simon Kenton. *Historical Marker Database.*

a man named Simon Girty told them that they were punishing Kenton and not Harrod.[229]

Most Kentuckians were as eager as Kenton to stand off against the Native Americans. Enrollment was increased, and the forts were in danger of being unmanned. The leaders worked out a plan that every fifth gun should stand guard at the forts, while the others went on to the Piqua (Pickaway) Indian town; Harrod organized his regiment quickly. He ordered every man to furnish his own provisions, and every sixth man formed a mess equipped with a pack horse to carry blankets, cook kettle, axe, parched corn, meat and salt. Each volunteer needed to supply his own bread for the first few days.[230]

Harrod and Logan were to rendezvous with Clark at the mouth of the Licking River. Harrod set out as soon he had organized his regiment, not even waiting to put in a supply of jerked meat. When they arrived, they found that there were not enough boats ready to carry men to the Licking River. Knowing that a delay would mean crisis, Harrod allowed his men to go on a two-day hunt. Finding food was harder than expected because the influx of people had frightened much of the game away. They were able to kill two buffalo and seven deer, hardly enough for their immediate needs.

To make up the loss, Hugh McGary suggested that Harrod take his company of thirty men across to the Indian side of the river to hunt along the shore as they marched to the rendezvous point. Harrod knew that this plan was risky, but he didn't oppose it because he knew that McGary had a hot temper.

When Clark learned what McGary did, he immediately ordered Harrod and his men back to the Kentucky side of the river. Before the order was carried out, McGary's company overpowered a large group of Native Americans from their shore side camp. As the white men were picking up their booty of deerskins and jerked meat, the Native Americans, trying to retreat, ran out of the bushes and killed nine white men. "This little attack put a stop to hunting on the shore."[231]

Provisions were low, but the men continued on. Near the mouth of the Licking River, they found a flatboat loaded with corn on the way to the falls for marketing. Clark bought the entire amount, and they divided the grain among the men. Since the grain was unmilled and not ready to use, the army had to stop while it was being processed.

Harrod arranged for each man to pound, parch or bake his share, and since many of the men had rotten teeth, most elected to grind the corn. He then ordered them to take the big axe from his pack horse and chop down an eight-inch oak sapling, square it off on one end and shave it to a point on the other. Next the men drove their hominy block into the ground and made a wooden pestle about three feet long. They took a piece of deerskin and wound it around the top. They poured their corn in, a pint at a time, and ground it. When one man tired, another took over. As the grain was ground, other men were heating salt water to add to the meal.[232]

While the men cooked the corn, others raised a cabin on the Indian side of the river to provide a place for guards, who were to keep their boats ready to go across to the Kentucky side in case of a hasty retreat.

The march up the Little Miami Valley was quick and uneventful. When the main force got within five miles of old Chillicothe, their spies returned with news that the Native Americans were deserting the town. In order to get there as soon as possible, the army hurried and reached the town, but they were too late. Native Americans had burned the buildings and vanished into the forest.

There was nothing they could do but march on up the Miami River to the Piqua town, reaching there by morning. There was a short skirmish, but it caused little damage to the white men or the Native Americans. As the troops took stock of the situation, they ventured out in different

A state highway marker for Little Miami Valley. *Historical Marker Database*.

An illustration of the attack at Vincennes.

directions. Harrod's men marched to flank Clark's men and attack the retreating Native Americans.

When Harrod's party reached the edge of the woods, the Native Americans fired, killing one of his men. Fighting broke out. The Native Americans had the advantage because they controlled an area full of ridges, but Harrod ordered his men to advance. They drove the Native Americans from tree to tree until, finally the Indians retreated to their fort, a triangular stockade covering half an acre of the town. Harrod knew that the Native American fort had recently been built in expectation of this attack.[233]

Harrod and the other commanders formed a hollow square, while a detachment rushed to the rear to bring up an old brass six-pounder cannon that the Illinois regiment had taken at Vincennes. They loaded the cannon and fired a dozen times into the fort. Finally, the Native Americans fled. The Kentuckians camped at the fort, with half of them on guard duty to monitor surprise attacks. In the aftermath, twenty men were dead and forty wounded; the pioneers took seventy-three Indian scalps.[234]

Chapter 9

1781–1782

Kentucky at a Crossroad

The thought of defeat had not entered anyone's mind, least of all Jim's.
—*Kathryn Harrod Mason,* James Harrod of Kentucky

I n the fall of 1780, Virginia did away with the county of Kentucky, setting up three new counties: Jefferson, Lincoln and Fayette. Jefferson County would now be "that part of the south side of the Kentucky River which lies west and north of a line beginning at the mouth of Benson's Big Creek and running up the same and its main fork to the head…south to the nearest waters of Hammond's Creek and down the same to its junction with the Town Fork of Salt River…south to Green River," northwest near the falls of the Ohio with the new chartered town of Louisville. Fayette would be "that part which lies north of the line beginning at the mouth of the Kentucky River, and up the same to its middle fork to the head…southwest to the Washington line" and the northeast around Boonesborough. (The present state of Tennessee was then known as the "District of Washington" belonging to North Carolina.) Lincoln County "embraced the residue of the original county of Kentucky," with Harrodsburg at its center.[235]

The government of these three counties in military matters was, according to Virginia law, entrusted to the county lieutenants: Ben Logan for Lincoln, John Todd for Fayette and John Floyd for Jefferson. This title was from the old English shire system and adapted for Virginia's government. The county lieutenants were men of affluence and, as head of civil government, were executive rather than judicial, with power to call out militia and order courts-martial.[236]

Kentucky's Original Three Counties

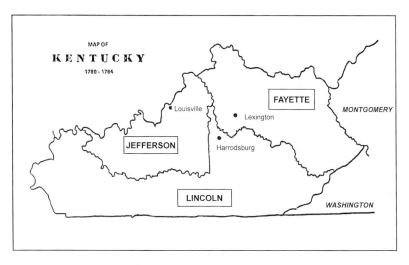

Fincastle County, Virginia – Formed 1772
Kentucky County, Virginia – Formed 1776
Kentucky County, Virginia - Divided in 1780

Jefferson, Lincoln, & Fayette Counties converge at the point Benson Creek flows into Kentucky River in downtown Frankfort.

A map of the original three counties in Kentucky: Lincoln, Jefferson and Fayette. *Kentucky Secretary of State Office.*

The governor appointed members of the county court. Early on, these were also men of substance and referred to as conservators of the peace. Each county appointed its own court clerk. Since there had been a huge influx of women into Kentucky during 1781, the first process issued by county clerks was a license to marry.[237]

The county clerks only had limited civil and criminal authority, with quarterly sessions to try and punish misdemeanors and felonies and resolve common-law and equity cases. The remainder of the judicial business was conducted at monthly sessions. However, they had no power to try capital cases. Capital cases were taken to Richmond. Harrod and his neighbors protested this in opening remarks of their 1780 petition to the Continental Congress.

In the second meeting of the 1781 Lincoln County Court, they discussed building a permanent meeting place because the blockhouse used at Fort

GRAVE OF JOHN FLOYD, NEAR
HERE. PIONEER AND SURVEYOR.
BORN AMHERST COUNTY, VA.,1750.
KILLED WHEN AMBUSHED BY INDIANS
IN JEFFERSON COUNTY, DISTRICT OF
KENTUCKY, 1783. COLONEL OF
MILITIA AND COUNTY LIEUTENANT
OF JEFFERSON COUNTY.

A state highway marker for John Floyd. *Historical Marker Database.*

Harrod was only a temporary location. Ben Logan saw the need early and made an offer of ten acres of his own land, including Buffalo Springs, for building a courthouse and other county buildings. The Buffalo Spring location would later become the city of Stanford.[238]

The first justices were loaded with orders for locating roads between the various stations, with settling the price of "spirituous liquors" and trying cases for horse racing and gambling. John Cowan caused a stir when he refused to take the oath of allegiance to Virginia, saying that he had already sworn oath to the United States. Overnight, he changed his mind and the next morning took his seat as a justice of Lincoln County.[239]

The cohesiveness of the settlers was strained from land disputes, the stress of continuing Native American warfare, the arguments about independence from Virginia and from recent arrivals of more Monongahela and eastern Pennsylvania settlers. Loyalties were forged with the three county governments.

As time went on, those from Lincoln County did not feel responsible for the communities along the Ohio River and refused to contribute the necessary support for Clark's regiment at the falls, thinking that they had enough trouble financing and recruiting men for their new county government. The other two counties soon agreed. There was justification for a stand because Clark, as highest-ranking military officer in Kentucky, had no regular authority over the county militias because his unit was part of a state organization.[240]

Indian raids during the summer of 1782 grew more frequent and dangerous. Spies told them of a British expedition planning to attack Logan's Station. At this same time, McAfee Station, seven miles from Fort Harrod, received a sudden attack. Harrod was not in town at the time, but Hugh McGary was and he heard the firing in the distance. He quickly rounded up some men and raced from Harrodstown to McAfee, yelling louder than the natives. Hearing their noisy approach, the Native Americans fled, fearing a large counterattack.

The Native American attacks were so bad that even the young boys had no time to be idle, and several of the older ones joined a company and went to help Bryan's Station when it was under siege. Harrod and the other leaders, fearing that Bryan's Station would not withstand a large attack, sent out companies from all the older stations. Boone led one from Boonesborough and Logan from his station. McGary led Harrodstown's company because at this time Harrod had lumbago and was confined to his house. Harrod never thought that his company could lose because they had more than 150 men. However, he was devastated to learn that the Native Americans won a big victory near the lower Blue Licks.

A state highway marker for the Buffalo Springs Courthouse. *Historical Marker Database.*

A state highway marker for Bryan's Station. *Historical Marker Database.*

McGary reached home the night after the Battle of Blue Licks and was the first to bring the news of the defeat. Draper drew a rough sketch of the ground plan of the "Harrodstown Fort" and added the following data:

Harrodstown Fort.
McGary. The Linns lived on the west side of L.
Harrod lived.
Edward Worthington
William Poague
Levi Todd
Benjamin Logan. Whitley. Clark. Manifee.

Logan, Whitley, Clark and Manifee lived on south side of the fort. A lad named John Miles went out near dark to get wood and was shot after the Blue Lick defeat. Levi and Robert Todd and John Todd—all lived there a while—Levi and John before they married, and Levi after.

But one big gate and that on the south side. Some two or more smaller ones. There was a stone wall around the spring. [Draper here drew a rough map of the fort and the surrounding grounds and under it wrote the following:]

The ground on which the fort was a rising eminence, descending in every way except the south.[241]

There were eight Harrodstown people killed at Blue Licks battle—Joseph Lindsay, James Brown, John Kennedy, Capt. Clough Overton, Stevens, and three others. Defeat August 19, 1782. Thinks eight or twelve were taken prisoner.

Hugh McGary. The people of Harrodstown used to consider McGary as a blustering and rather cowardly man. Mrs. Thomas recollects seeing John Gordon make McGary run.[242]

Pioneer women of Bryan Station facing Indians in ambush with heroic courage and sublime self-sacrifice.

A historical postcard from Harrodsburg's 150th anniversary celebration depicting the pioneer women from Bryan's Station. *Author's personal collection.*

"SO VALIANTLY DID OUR SMALL PARTY FIGHT THAT,
TO THE MEMORY OF THOSE WHO UNFORTUNATELY FELL
IN THE BATTLE, ENOUGH OF HONOUR CANNOT BE PAID."
--- DANIEL BOONE

COLONEL-COMMANDANT
JOHN TODD (KILLED)

LIEUTENANT-COLONELS
DANIEL BOONE   STEPHEN TRIGG (KILLED)

MAJORS
EDWARD BULGER   SILAS HARLAN
(DIED OF WOUNDS)   (KILLED)
HUGH McGARY   LEVI TODD

CAPTAINS
JOHN ALLISON   JOHN BEASLEY (CAPTURED)
JOHN BULGER (KILLED) JOHN GORDON (KILLED)
SAMUEL JOHNSON   JOSEPH KINCAID (KILLED)
GABRIEL MADISON   WILLIAM McBRIDE (KILLED)
CLOUGH OVERTON (KILLED) ROBERT PATTERSON

LIEUTENANTS
WILLIAM GIVINS (KILLED) THOMAS HINSON (KILLED)
JOHN KENNEDY (KILLED)   JAMES McGUIRE (KILLED)
BARNETT ROGERS (KILLED)

ENSIGN
JOHN McMURTRY (CAPTURED)

COMMISSARY
JOSEPH LINDSAY (KILLED)

DEDICATED AUGUST 19, 1928

THIS MONUMENT, THE GIFT OF A GRATEFUL COMMONWEALTH, COMMEMORATES
THE HEROIC PIONEERS, WHO, IN DEFENCE OF KENTUCKY, HERE FOUGHT AND FELL,
IN THE BATTLE OF THE BLUE LICKS, AUGUST 19, 1782

The Blue Licks Monument listing the pioneer command structure. *Kentucky Kindred Genealogy, Phyllis Brown.*

"THEY ADVANCED IN THREE DIVISIONS, IN GOOD ORDER,
AND GAVE US A VOLLEY AND STOOD TO IT VERY WELL
FOR SOME TIME."
— WILLIAM CALDWELL

PRIVATES
WHO ESCAPED

THOMAS ACRES
WILLIAM
 ALDRIDGE
ELIJAH ALLEN
JAMES ALLEN
ABRAHAM
 BOWMAN
ROBERT
 BOWMAR
THOMAS
 BROOKS
JAMES COBURN
 WOUNDED
JACOB
 GOFFMAN
JOSEPH
 COLLINS
EDWARD CORN
WILLIAM
 CUSTER
RICHARD
 DAVIS
THEODORUS
 DAVIS
PETER DIERLY
THOMAS
 FICKLIN
HENRY FRENCH
HENRY GRIDER
JEREMIAH
 GULLION

WILLIAM BARBEE
SQUIRE BOONE, JR.
 (WOUNDED)
GEORGE CORN
WHITFIELD CRAIG
THOMAS GIST
JAMES GRAHAM
PETER HARGET
JAMES M. JANUARY
WAINRIGHT LEA
JAMES McCULLOUGH
ANDREW MORGAN
JOHN MORGAN
JOHN PITMAN
AARON REYNOLDS
LEWIS ROSE (CAPTURED)
JOSEPH SCHOLL
SAMUEL SCOTT
ANDREW STEELE
THOMAS STEVENSON
JAMES SWART
JAMES TWYMAN
JAMES ELIJAH WOODS
 (CAPTURED)
BARTLETT SEARCY
JOHN SEARCY
WILLIAM SHOTT
ANTHONY SOWDUSKY
JOHN SUMMERS

SAMUEL BOONE
BENJAMIN A. COOPER
JERRY CRAIG
WILLIAM FIELD
EDWARD GRAHAM
SQUIRE GRANT
BENJAMIN HAYDEN
JAMES KINCAID
JAMES McBRIDE
WILLIAM MAY
JAMES MORGAN
 (CAPTURED BUT ESCAPED)
BENJAMIN NETHERLAND
JAMES RAY
JAMES ROSE
ABRAHAM SCHOLL
PETER SCHOLL
JOHN SMITH
JACOB STEVENS
JACOB STUCKER
HENRY WILSON
JESSE YOCUM
 (CAPTURED)
ROBERT SCOTT
GEORGE SMITH
SAMUEL SHORTRIDGE
EDMUND SINGLETON
JOSIAH WILSON
SAMUEL WOODS

JOHN
 HAMBLETON
JOHN HART
JAMES HAYS
JAMES HARROD
HENRY HIGGINS
JOHN HINCH
CHARLES
 HUNTER
JACOB HUNTER
EPHRAIM
 JANUARY
WILLIAM LAM
JOHN LITTLE
JAMES
 McCONNELL
MORDECAI
 MORGAN
HENRY NIXON
JAMES NORTON
MATTHEW
 PATTERSON
JOHN PEAKE
ALEXANDER
 PENLIN
ROBERT
 POAGUE
ELISHA PRUETT
ANDREW RULE

WYANDOTS AND MINGOES

The Blue Licks Monument listing the soldiers. *Kentucky Kindred Genealogy, Phyllis Brown.*

Because of the confusion with the survivors, many blamed Major McGary for the defeat. Maddened by the delay, McGary swore that he had come for a fight and splashed across the river, calling all who would not follow him "damn cowards." The more experienced fighters wanted to wait for Logan's reinforcements before facing the Native Americans, but McGary and his men rushed across the Licking River to death and disaster.[243]

The Native Americans killed more than 60 white men but lost only 6 of their own. On August 24, Colonel Logan and 470 men arrived in time to bury the slain. Daniel Boone reported the horror to be almost unparalleled: "We...found their bodies strewed everywhere, cut and mangled in a dreadful manner....Some torn and eaten by wild beasts; those in the river eaten by fishes; all in such a putrefied condition that none could be distinguished from another."[244]

The effect of this loss was immediate and violent. The panic was so great that even the oldest settlers declared that they were returning to their former homes. One settler said that he offered his father the entire 1,400 acres of his preemption for a horse to carry his family back to Virginia.[245]

With the exception of the loss of life, one of the greatest tragedies was the aftermath of the attack. Todd and McGary received the majority of the blame. Todd was accused of being too anxious to prove his military skills and McGary chided for his rashness in leading the charge. McGary became the most hated man in Kentucky. Harrod often said that if he had been along, he could have stopped McGary before it was too late.[246]

Clark acted immediately. He had been promoted to a higher authority from the governor to prepare a large offensive expedition in Kentucky. He called a meeting of the militia officers— including Harrod, Logan and Floyd— to sit on a council to outline plans for a retaliatory attack. They feared that the disaster at Blue Licks might make a military draft necessary in order to get enough recruits. The ambush had devastated one-thirteenth of Kentucky's militia. Many settlers fled back east, leaving the west open for more attacks and causing 1782 to be remembered as the "Year of Blood."[247]

A state highway marker Blue Licks Battlefield. *Historical Marker Database.*

In late September, more than one thousand men—under the command of Harrod, Logan, Floyd and several others—gathered on the banks of the Ohio River at the mouth of the Licking River to meet Clark. On this latest attempt to capture Detroit, Clark took every precaution to make his expedition successful. He gave detailed plans for the mark and strict orders for discipline. Harrod and the others maintained the line throughout the six-day march along a quickly cut path.

The Kentuckians moved the Native Americans northward, taking seven prisoners and liberating two white men, but the Native Americans were staying far away from the battle. The settlers burned crops and destroyed ten thousand bushels of the Native Americans' winter corn. The pioneers collected all the blankets, kettles and guns that were gathered for sale later at auction. Eventually, the army of settlers went home, although they still wanted revenge for the loss at Blue Licks.

The order was given to return home because bad weather was advancing and it was too dangerous to continue on to Detroit. Although they didn't take Detroit, the expedition did have several accomplishments. The Native Americans were now in panic mode, as their winter supplies were gone. The British believed that the Long Knives had more men than they actually did. Sickness was widespread, and the Native Americans, with decreased support from the British, realized the hopelessness of winning against the Kentuckians. Finally, the confidence the pioneers had lost because of the massacre at Blue Lick was restored. Harrod realized that the people gained many new recruits who had come to the Bluegrass as promised.[248]

Chapter 10

1783–1784

The First Courts at Harrodstown

For the first time, Harrod's settlers enjoyed an era of comparative peace.
—*Kathryn Harrod Mason,* James Harrod of Kentucky

During the two years following Clark's 1782 campaign, only a few raiding parties came to the dark and bloody ground. Families could finally return to their clearing, fence in more land, repair neglected plows and build new cabins for growing families. Children could play without fear throughout the settlement. Wives could venture alone from the clearing to gather rotted nettles for weaving or help with sugar making at the Shawnee springs.[249]

As soon as settlers could move outside the safety of the fort, the training of racehorses was started as a business and for entertainment and diversion. In 1783, a racetrack was started in Harrodstown, and it was named "Haggin's Race Path." Soon after, Hugh McGary was fined for betting on horse races at this track. This racetrack soon had competition from a racecourse started on Race Street in Fayette County.[250]

With the ending of the Revolutionary War and near elimination of hostile Native American activity, the Ohio River became the preferred entry route into Kentucky. The Bluegrass Region was soon settled with a mix of early settlers, land speculators and veterans who received land grants in lieu of back pay. The process of taking a land grant and receiving a legal deed of ownership involved endless property line disputes. This litigation arguably created more lawyers per capita in Kentucky than any other state.[251]

There were signs of renewed civil activity and increased demand for more self-government. By the spring of 1783, Virginia had restored Kentucky as a district and set up a high court system that could finally handle capital cases. Harrod turned his attention to family. Ann was homesick for old friends and relatives in North Carolina; her son, James, was nine years old, and she wanted to show him off. She was also upset because she had not conceived a baby with Harrod.[252]

Harrod was happiest when he had children around him. His nephews Thomas, William Harrod Jr. and James Harrod, his namesake, had been living at Boiling Spring for several years. Since the death of John Harrod Jr. a few days after Christmas 1781, his wife had been sending messages trying to get Harrod to bring twenty-year-old Thomas back to Bedford, so he could look after her and his sisters. So, while Ann Harrod was visiting with her family in North Carolina, her husband left to bring Thomas home.

Upon his return to Kentucky, Harrod turned his thoughts to the establishment of the new district court and his seat on the grand jury. He heard cases on the selling of spirituous liquors without a license, adultery, fornication and the irregularity on the part of the Lincoln County clerk. The first court met at Harrodstown, but because there was no adequate building, the justices authorized a new one to be built. The court was temporarily at Crow's station, not far from Boiling Spring, near the Town Spring in present-day Danville. The new building was large enough to have a courtroom at one end and two jury rooms at the other. They also built a jail of hewed, sawed logs at least nine inches thick.[253]

The Treaty of Paris was supposed to stop the native fighting, but ratification was slow and the Native Americans still found British to maintain their fur trade and help. The terms of the treaty were to be that Great Britain would relinquish posts along the Great Lakes and withdraw supplies that enabled the Native Americans. So, the Native Americans could not make large-scale attacks against Kentucky, but they could make sharp hits at the weakly fortified and inadequately smaller settlements.[254]

The resurgence of Native American attacks damaged Kentucky both spiritually and physically. During the early hard years, the Kentucky pioneers had come to expect danger. Now that the war was over, they wanted peace and security. Virginia did not want to sanction raids into native country since it was about to relinquish to the national government the Ohio and Great Lakes. Kentucky could not get permission for an offense from Congress because the delegates wanted to temporarily appease the Native Americans.[255]

The William Crow House at Crow Station near Boiling Spring. *Library of Congress.*

In November 1784, Benjamin Logan called the leading men of Jefferson County to Danville to see what could be done about the continued Native American problem. Spies from the south had warned him that the Cherokees and Chickamaugas were holding a great council and about to send out a large war party to attack Kentucky. Although there was imminent physical danger, politics also entered the discussions.

The assembly soon realized that it had no claim for calling out the militia to be used offensively, nor was there any magazine to provide powder and bullets for the expedition. Because this was officially a time of peace, Kentucky could no longer support supplies for a new campaign. As it turned out, the alarm was for nothing. Even though this news was either a false alarm or an abandoned project, the meeting did bring attention to Kentucky's weak position.[256]

The war was over, but Harrod was still concerned about the danger from the Native Americans. The delegates called another formal convention to meet a few days after Christmas 1784. They elected a president and a clerk and started to transact business. In the first formal Danville convention, old and new grievances were aired: unequal taxation, inefficient administration of justice, lack of provisions for calling out the militia, the drainage of money to the east, the double allegiance to Virginia and the national government.

Only one resolution was recorded: a complaint against a special tax levied on estates of 1,400 or more acres. It was carried by a vote of twenty to ten, with Harrod voting yes, along with the land speculators.[257]

The statehood separation was brought up for discussion because, up to this point, Kentucky had been dependent on Virginia. Kentucky now had two types of settlers: the early pioneers from Virginia whose claims were by preemption rights or military warrants and all the newcomers from Pennsylvania and the east who tried to get land with treasury warrants. Some of the bolder members questioned why Kentucky should continue to be loyal to the easterners, who were too willing to take advantage of pioneers. The long-suffering Kentuckians listened to the argument but were unaware of the forces wanting to take Kentucky out of the Union. Spain had conspirators in the west, and they were eager to hear from the separatists.[258]

Harrod was eager. His new land had cost too much in blood and labor to let it be a pawn in national politics. He believed that the pioneers' best interest would be a complete break from Virginia. Harrod wanted statehood for Kentucky.

When he returned to Harrodstown, James and his neighbors petitioned the Virginia legislature to legally establish their town, with 140 townspeople signing the petition. They thought the survey of 640 acres of land that the House of Delegates had formerly reserved for the use of the garrison and town of Harrodstown was the most convenient and suitable in the country.[259]

By the fall of 1785, the Virginia legislature had passed an act establishing Harrodstown as Harrodsburg and providing for the survey and purchase of lots for setting up a governing body of trustees, which included Harrod, Abraham Chaplin, Benjamin Logan and nine others. The trustees met the following March and defined boundaries for the public lands, allowing people already living in the settlement until December next to pay for the lands they wished to occupy at the rate of ten shillings per acre, with the stipulation that if the purchasers chose, they would have the liberty of sowing grain at any time after November next.[260]

Chapter 11

1785–1786

THE CIVILIZATION OF KENTUCKY

The stream of immigration was on the increase and many home seekers
and land speculators came to Harrodstown.
—*Mary A. Stephenson, "Some Early Industries of Mercer County,"*
Register of Kentucky State Historical Society

I t now was becoming respectable for families to move to the new frontier. The Revolution had ended, there was a new district court and the division of Kentucky into three separate counties gave the western country a sense of stability. "Such has been the progress of the settlement of this country, from dirty stations or forts, and smoky huts, [to] blushing orchards, pleasant gardens, luxuriant sugar groves, neat and commodious houses, sifing [*sic*] villages and trading town. Ten years have produced a difference in the population and comforts of this country, which to be pourtrayed in just colours would appear marvellous."[261]

Up until now, most of the immigrants came from Virginia, Maryland, North Carolina and Pennsylvania, but now the west was calling to a new set of pioneers from New England and even Europe. At first, the newcomers were speculators or journalists wanting to exploit the backwoodsmen and their adventures. For the first time in Kentucky, young women arrived in large numbers. This was an indication that the west was no longer beyond the periphery of civilization.

One sign of civilization was the opening of a dry goods store in Louisville in 1783. Settlers could buy many forgotten luxuries and most of their

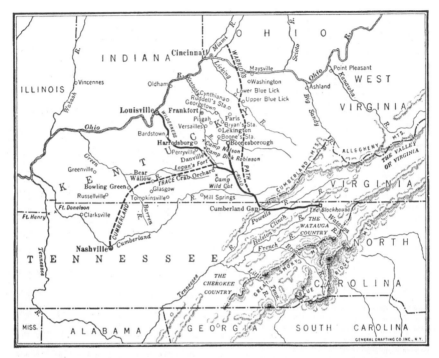

MAP OF PIONEER ROADS

A map of the original pioneer roads.

necessities. The son of William Harrod's old Fort Pitt commander, Dan Broadhead, was the owner of the large business.[262] The store was a double cabin, and he displayed silks, satins, broadcloths and other finery brought across the country. He also sold dry goods, groceries, hardware, furniture and anything else the pioneers needed.[263]

Ann Harrod and her friends found any excuse to visit Broadhead's store. Bartering was a well-established policy in Kentucky, so for people with little money, they brought linsey, maple sugar, tobacco, pork, corn, whiskey or dried skins to barter. James would often stop at the store after a hunting trip to buy Ann a clothing pattern or a yard of lace she had asked for. Ann was also fond of candlesticks, candle molds and silver spoons.[264]

Boiling Spring Station had become a regular stopping place for Virginia land speculators, and Harrod wanted to provide a few refinements. His house had simple furnishings but included more than a dozen books and a few pieces of queen's ware and Delftware, a blue and white pottery made in and around Delft in the Netherlands. James no longer had to go to Fort Pitt to buy rifles and accessories because good gunsmiths were setting up business in Harrodsburg and Louisville.[265]

Harrod was the first person in Kentucky to set up a beehive. Because the new settlers loved sweets, they went to some trouble in order to get them. On one trip to the Tenmile country, he harvested bee gum, which is a portion of a hollow gum tree where honeybees set up hives. He loaded it onto his boat and brought the hive home. Word traveled very fast, and the settlers from

A state highway marker for Isaac Selby's home Traveler's Rest. *Historical Marker Database.*

all over Bluegrass came to buy honey in Harrodsburg. It is said that Isaac Shelby, a Tennessee pioneer and the future first governor of Kentucky, paid Harrod a cow and a calf for honey.[266]

A small baby boom was happening in Kentucky at this time. James and Ann had been married seven years with no children of their own, but finally in September 1785, Margaret Harrod was born, Ann's second child and the only child of her second marriage. There have been questions pertaining to the paternity of Margaret, with some believing she was not Harrod's child at all. The manager of Harrod's farm was often seen around the house. The man's name was Mahon, and he had red hair, just like Margaret; Harrod's hair was black. One pioneer, Colonel Nathaniel Hart, said that Ann had acknowledged to him that James was not the father. However, Harrod never made mention of this, claimed Margaret as his own and was as devoted to her as he was to his stepson.[267]

Margaret was named for Ann's mother, Margaret Coburn. Because of her interest in education, Ann opened the Harrod Latin School in 1786 at their home. A Latin teacher, Mr. Worley, was imported to the station for the education of Harrod's stepson James, as well as other students who came from the surrounding fortifications to dwell with Harrod. Another of the students was John Fauntleroy, then eight years of age, who would later marry Margaret and become Harrod's son-in-law. In November 1787, young James McDaniel wandered off into the woods, where he was taken by Native Americans and burned at the stake. Harrod's grievous mourning was inconsolable after the tragic loss of his adored stepson, and as he was unable to bear the sight and sounds of the dead boy's classmates, he closed the Latin School.[268]

Young Fauntleroy finished his education in Lexington, but he later returned to Harrodsburg to marry Margaret Harrod. Margaret died on August 25, 1841, at Boiling Spring at the age of nearly fifty-six years, leaving a large number of worthy descendants. Ann Harrod lived most of her adult years at Boiling Spring and died there on April 14, 1843, in her eighty-eighth year. She was among the very last of the venerable pioneer women of Kentucky.

Many ministers resisted moving west because of reports of the coldness to religion shown by the settlers. This religious indifference was overlooked when it became apparent that a preacher could become prosperous in Kentucky. However, this wealth could prove embarrassing when a devotee of the gospel was up for congregational election. Sometimes a preacher would be criticized because of the fineness of his coat, but if he had the right amount of humility, he could fend off criticism. Presbyterian minister Father David Rice married more couples than any minister in early Kentucky. He could also pray and chew tobacco with equal vigor, sending a fine brown spray through the open door without soiling a bonnet.[269]

Although Harrod followed no particular religion, he recognized the importance of establishing churches in his community. Reverend John Shane, an early Kentucky historian, recorded that Harrod held his house open to public worship. Religious fervor increased through the years, and Harrod's house continued to serve as the chapel because it was large enough to hold the entire worship assembly in comfort.

The Methodist Church held its first quarterly conference at Boiling Spring in 1786. According to Ann Harrod, sixty-five "worshippers gathered around the hearth" and many passionate services were held. There were many converts; Ann "became a devout and influential member of the Methodist congregation."[270]

Harrod wanted a large landed estate for his heirs, which were now only Ann and Margaret after the death of his stepson in 1787. Possessing many acres was a symbol of pride to Harrod, and he owned a large amount of land: 1,300 acres at Boiling Spring, 1,400 acres in Lincoln County, 18,000 acres in Jefferson County and 700 acres in Mercer County. He also surveyed 200,000 to 300,000 acres in the Green River country, but he lost most of this due to inadequate paperwork.[271]

Interest in land was shifting to the Ohio River tracts opposite the falls, where Harrod's brother William was securing land under George Rogers Clark's Illinois grant. The officers and soldiers were to receive 150,000 acres in reward for their service. This land was on the Native American side of the Ohio River. William, as captain of the Illinois Regiment, was entitled to 3,000 acres. Because he was unable to appear and claim his land, James wrote a letter to Clark. The following is the only surviving letter written by James Harrod:

Dr Sir,

As Opportunity will not admit of my attending to the Claime of Wm. Harrod—I hope you will oblige me So Fare as to quit out his Surtificate and If there is a Lottery be kind anuf to attend his Drafts. I Expect my Brother will be at the falls Every Day and if he—Should be Disapointed from Coming I will pay you for aney Expence that may arise from it.

Pray oblige your Hble Servant.
James Harrod Aprile 25, 1785.[272]

Harrod and many of the first pioneers had to prove their prior claims against later arrivals, mainly through testimony of fellow settlers. Most did not have any documentary evidence. Sometimes these cases went to the court of appeals or the Supreme Court. Logan and Harrod were codefendants as well as opponents in several land title cases. Daniel Boone's suit against Harrod started in September 1788 and went through twenty-three continuations until its dismissal in 1793.[273]

One of the most famous lawsuits was *Harrod v. Crow*. Harrod's heirs sued William Crow, whose station near Danville housed Transylvania College, the first college in the west, and the temporary courthouse. While Crow had been in the wilderness with Harrod in 1774 and 1775, he had taken land that the heirs claimed was contained in Harrod's first surveys. The case dragged through court for years before being settled in favor of Margaret Harrod. She gained the title to large valuable tracts of Danville land, which she sold at nominal prices to settlers there.[274]

Harrod had many duties that kept him tied to civilization and away from his favorite hunting ground. Three new counties were added to Kentucky in 1785: Mercer, Madison and Bourbon. Harrod served on the jury and acted as arbitrator and witness for countless court proceedings in Mercer and Lincoln Counties. During the fall of 1785 and through the summer of 1786, Kentuckians' idea for statehood was gaining support. There were many who were pushing for complete and immediate independence from the Union, although the majority of settlers still looked eastward to Virginia for authority.[275]

In August 1785, Danville's third convention sent a petition to Virginia to set a date for a late summer meeting. The delegates unanimously decided that it was the duty of the convention to make application to the General Assembly to ask for separation from the parent government, on terms honorable to both and harmful to neither. Virginia passed the Enabling Act, which required a fourth convention about statehood, scheduled for September 1786.[276]

Present Harrodsburg was the county seat of the last convention until Mercer County was formed in 1785, named after another Revolutionary War hero, General Hugh Mercer. Also in 1785, residents in Harrod's settlement drew up a petition to be submitted to the Virginia legislature, stating their compliance with the requirements of the latest land act, listing the natural advantages of the site and requesting that the "Honorable House would take the whole into consideration, [and] pass an Act for conveying the same to freeholders and other citizens in a manner most agreeable to your wisdom and determination."[277]

The document bore the signatures of 140 men. At the October session of 1785, the Virginia Assembly established the town, which was to be "known by the name of Harrodsburg, in the county of Lincoln." The act confirmed its right to a 640-acre tract. It named thirteen trustees, who were authorized to dispense maximum half-acre in-lots (for residence) and ten-acre out-lots (for pasturage and farming) to persons of just claim and sell the balance. All persons acquiring in-lots were required to "erect and build thereon a dwelling-house of the dimensions of twenty feet by sixteen, at the least, with a brick or stone chimney," within a period of three years or else the trustees could repossess the property and dispose of it "for the best price that can be got and apply the money arising therefrom to the use and advantage of the said town." The trustees also could "cause an accurate survey to be made of the said township." With the official nod from Williamsburg, the town could now take on definitive form.

However, the fourth convention was delayed and was not able to meet until January 1787.[278]

Chapter 12

1787–1792

Onward to Statehood

It was expedient for, and the will of the good people of the district to separate from the state of Virginia and become an independent state.
—*Lowell H. Harrison,* Kentucky's Road to Statehood

By the spring of 1786, Benjamin Logan and James Harrod were again riding to George Rogers Clark's side to combat the Native Americans in the Ohio Valley. Logan marshaled men to attack a Shawnee town as a diversion while Clark moved against the Wabashes. The Shawnees were taken completely unaware, and Harrod captured the chief, Moluntha, who had been the victor at the Battle of Blue Lick. Moluntha had his horse packed and was ready to flee, so he shielded himself, but tragedy happened. Hotheaded Hugh McGary sank an axe blade into Moluntha's skull before anyone could stop him. Many historians feel that McGary took this action as revenge for being embarrassed at Blue Lick.[279]

Harrod was forced to hold a court-martial when they returned to Harrodsburg, although he would not be at the court proceedings. Hugh McGary was charged with disobedience for killing a prisoner of war, insulting and abusing other officers, declaring that he would kill any man who tried to keep him from killing the chief and conduct unbecoming a gentleman and officer. The court decided that McGary was guilty of murdering Moluntha, and his character was unbecoming an officer. He was suspended from active service for one year.[280]

After these events, Harrod returned to Boiling Spring to enjoy his new house, family and farm. All around it was rich land filled with crops, and enslaved laborers worked in the fields. He cherished his feather beds, which were filled with the feathers of geese from the farm. He also had twenty-eight sheep to give them wool for clothing, twenty milk cows and eighteen hogs for food. They also had plates and chairs for a dozen guests at meals.[281]

During the following years, Harrod was accused of excessive drinking. One pioneer stated that Harrod would get drunk when gambling and lose as much as $5,000 at one sitting. In 1786, drinking was an accepted practice. "Every man was obliged to keep a kind of grog shop in his home, for his neighbors, acquaintances, and hangers on."[282] A whiskey bottle was always passed around at house-raisings or corn-huskings; liquor was considered an incentive to labor.[283]

Statehood was still a hot topic among the settlers. Some of the pioneers wanted radical separation from Virginia, even without statehood, while the rest wanted to follow the written law. The latter group moved slowly from convention to convention, hoping that the orderly action would better serve Kentucky's interests and welfare.

During the tenth and final Danville convention in 1792, they drew up their constitution. One group favored slavery and property rights, and another group advocated for a one-house legislature, voting by ballot and opposing slavery. The resulting compromise was progressive democracy and staid conservatism with similarities to the new U.S. Constitution.[284]

On June 1, 1792, the Commonwealth of Kentucky was admitted into the Union as the fifteenth state. Kentucky granted suffrage to all free men over the age of twenty-one. Representation was now based on population instead of territorial units. Elections were to be held annually, and there was a guarantee of religious freedom. It had been eighteen years since James Harrod had founded Harrodstown, and the rough census in 1792 was over 100,000 people.[285]

Harrod was not much for politics, so he would frequently sneak off to go hunting or trapping. Game was becoming scarce because Kentucky was filling up with settlers. Having grown up in the wilderness, Harrod was not suited for civilized life. When court concluded for the season, he would leave for long hunting trips, usually alone and for several months. He always wore a broad-brimmed beaver hat, jeans and a hunting shirt trimmed with initialed silver buttons.[286]

A log cabin replica in Constitution Square Park, Danville. *Keith Rightmyer*.

The Governor's Monument in Constitution Square Park. *Keith Rightmyer*.

A replica of the district courthouse in Constitution Square Park. *Keith Rightmyer.*

Sometime in February 1792, James Harrod left on his last hunting expedition, and he never returned. According to his wife, Harrod was going with a man named Bridges to look for the lost Swift's silver mine. Jonathan Swift was a pirate, Native American trader, miner and smuggler. His lost silver mine inspired many people of the time to explore, dig and search for the treasures. Ann was afraid for Harrod's safety because Bridges was in a contested lawsuit with Harrod, so she encouraged her husband to take Michael Stoner with him.[287]

When James Harrod failed to appear for the last Danville convention, there was only gossip and rumors about his disappearance; no one knows the real reason. He was perhaps killed by the Native Americans, he got sick and died of natural causes, he had a tragic accident or he was treacherously murdered by his companions. The latter was strongly suspected at the time, and his widow, only daughter and much later his son-in-law always thought Harrod fell by an assassin's hand. No matter the reason, James Harrod perished at about fifty years of age as one of the noblest of the pioneer fathers of Kentucky. He never knew that his efforts to make Kentucky a state in the Union became a reality.[288]

Of all the sons of John and Sarah Harrod, James Harrod was the one most devoted to family. Ann and his only living child, Margaret, who was seven years old when James disappeared, waited a year before giving up hope. Harrod's will had been made on November 28, 1791, before the

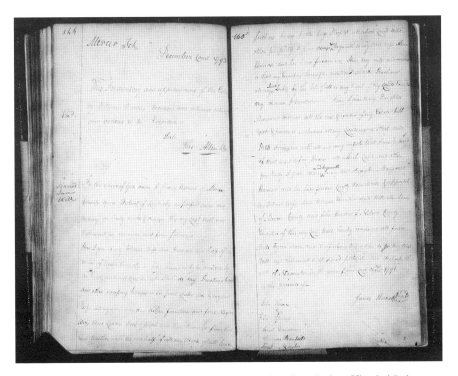

A photocopy of James Harrod's will from the *Register of the Kentucky State Historical Society*, January 1939. *Kentucky Historical Society*.

fateful trip. It was probated in December 1793. Harrod willed his entire estate to Ann and Margaret. An inventory showed personal items valued at more than £400 in addition to his vast land acquisitions.[289]

Because his body was never found, Harrod's disappearance gave rise to wild speculations and was the subject of malicious gossip. The records reveal that Harrod's death was accepted by his family, responsible members of the community, his associates, the law and his siblings. His seat on the Harrodsburg Board of Trustees was declared vacant on August 13, 1793. His will was produced before the open Court of Mercer County on August 27, 1793, and was recorded on January 28, 1794. Ann Harrod's testimony comes the closest to solving the mystery of Colonel Harrod's death: "Her husband was killed or died in a hunting expedition up the Kentucky River in the fall of the year 1792, and he had not been heard of since, a part of his clothing being found afterwards in the river."[290]

The marker at the Pioneer Cemetery at Old Fort Harrod pays homage to James Harrod:

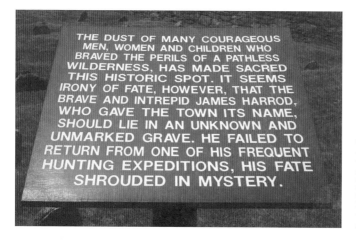

THE DUST OF MANY COURAGEOUS MEN, WOMEN AND CHILDREN WHO BRAVED THE PERILS OF A PATHLESS WILDERNESS, HAS MADE SACRED THIS HISTORIC SPOT. IT SEEMS IRONY OF FATE, HOWEVER, THAT THE BRAVE AND INTREPID JAMES HARROD, WHO GAVE THE TOWN ITS NAME, SHOULD LIE IN AN UNKNOWN AND UNMARKED GRAVE. HE FAILED TO RETURN FROM ONE OF HIS FREQUENT HUNTING EXPEDITIONS, HIS FATE SHROUDED IN MYSTERY.

The marker at the Pioneer Cemetery at Old Fort Harrod paying homage to James Harrod. *Keith Rightmyer.*

The dust of many courageous men, women and children, who braved the perils of a pathless wilderness, has made sacred this historic spot. It seems irony of fate, however, that the brave and intrepid James Harrod, who gave the town its name, should lie in an unknown and unmarked grave. He failed to return from one of his frequent hunting expeditions, his fate shrouded in mystery.[291]

Almost ten years after Harrod's disappearance, in late 1802, Ann remarried.[292] There is no record of her life after marrying a Mr. Tablock, but seven months after marrying Tablock, Ann sought to have the marriage dissolved because she stated that James Harrod was alive.[293] There are no records of her comments at this time, but the following is Ann Harrod's declaration before the Commonwealth of Kentucky in Boyle County in December 1843:

In the 3rd day of December 1842 personally appeared before me a justice of the peace for said county, Mrs. Ann Harrod, a resident of said county and state, aged eighty-six years and at this time infirm and confined to her bed, and unable to attend in open court, who first being duly sworn according to law, doth on her oath make the following declaration in order to obtain the benefit of the provisions made by the act of Congress passed July 4, 1836:[294]

That she is the widow of Colonel James Harrod, who was a Captain in the Virginia Militia in the year 1776 and in that capacity with a company of men explored a part of the State of Kentucky on the waters of Salt River and Kentucky River in the year 1774, and at that time laid off a town and built four or five cabins on the ground where the town of Harrodsburg is built: That in the month of July in that year his company had by the Native Americans one man killed at a large spring called Fountain Bleu three miles northwest of their town by the name of James Cowan which compelled them to retract back to Holston in Virginia where many of them resided, and soon after he raised a volunteer militia company which was called into service by the Governor of Virginia for three months and marched with Colonel Lewis to the Battle of the Point at the mouth of the Great Kanawha and performed his duty as her husband often told her; That he was honorably discharged; That in the spring of 1775 Harrod returned to Kentucky and erected with the aid of the then Captain McGary a fort at that place of which Harrod had the principal command; That this deponent moved to Kentucky with her husband, she being then married to a Mr. James McDonald, in the fall of the year 1775; that next year, 1776, her said husband was killed by the Native Americans, and she removed to Colonel Logan's Fort; that James Harrod continued in the command of the Fort at Harrodsburg, and in the fall of the year 1779, her then husband, James Harrod moved to her present residence Harrod's Station, six miles above and south of Harrodsburg, at which place her husband still commanded as Captain, and in the summer of 1780 commanded as Colonel, Colonel Logan not being present, on Colonel Ben Logan's Expedition against the Native Americans at Pickaway on the Big Miami; That from the fall of 1775 until the close of the Revolutionary War in 1783, Harrod was in continual service and in nearly all the skirmishes and attacks made by the Native Americans around Harrodsburg, during all of which time he was in command as a Captain at the Fort in Harrodsburg; That the fact of his being a captain will appear from the records in Richmond in Virginia, his old company book and his commission which was given to a Mr. W. H. Todd to procure the back pay of her husband and either filed in Richmond or in the Pension Office Washington City; She farther states that her husband was a captain and commissioned officer in constant service in the Virginia State Line from the date of this commission until the close of the Revolutionary War, about which time or not long after he was promoted to a Colonel's commission; She farther declares that she was married to Captain James Harrod in February of 1778, and that her husband was killed or died in a hunting expedition up the Kentucky River in the fall of 1792, and he has not been heard of since; a part of his clothes being found afterwards in the river; and that she has remained a widow ever since that period as will more fully appear by reference to the proof herewith annexed, except for the found months I was united to a man, but we were regularly divorced and I was restored to my former name Ann Harrod, and have been known as the widow of James Harrod for the 38 years last past. ~~Ann Harrod [295]

When Ann died in April 1843, she had resided on the same farm in Boiling Spring for more than sixty-three years and had been in Kentucky sixty-eight years. In the closing months of her life, she was found daily meditating on a tranquil expectation of death. [296]

Appendix

INCIDENTAL INFORMATION
REGARDING JAMES HARROD

The SS James Harrod *was lost in collision with American ship*
SS Raymond B. Stevens *in 1945.*
—Harrodsburg Herald, *June 25, 1948*

THE SS *JAMES HARROD*

The SS *James Harrod* Liberty Ship was named for the founder of Harrodsburg, Kentucky, and was launched on March 2, 1943, at Portland, Oregon, by the Oregon Shipbuilding Company. This 144th Liberty Ship, designated EC2-S-Cl, was completed during World War II. Its call sign was KKRQ. Constructed of steel, the SS *James Harrod* was a steam-powered vessel. At the launching program, a telegram was read from Harrodsburg mayor pro tem Tom Squifflet, acting while Mayor Maurice Watts was serving in the U.S. Navy. The telegram carried the appreciation of the citizens of Harrodsburg for the ship's name and expressed good wishes for the crew and the hope of a useful future for the gallant ship.[297]

Armed Guard Officer A.A. Hoehling was assigned to lead the gun crew on merchant ships. Beginning in December 1943, he began a series of voyages that took him to India, Singapore, Mozambique, Italy and Algeria, as well as various ports of the United Kingdom and the United States. He described his impressions of each port in captivating detail, from the exotic Kolkata (Calcutta) and Algiers to the uneasy neutrality of Laurenco

The SS *James Harrod* Liberty Ship. *Deal Library*.

The SS *James Harrod* after the ship was grounded. *David Chamberland*.

The SS *James Harrod* after the fire. *Deal Library*.

Marques to the bomb-damaged London, Liverpool and Southampton. Due to circumstances he alludes to but does not specify, he chose not to reveal the name of his first Liberty ship, referring to it instead by the pseudonym *John Lesher*. After a period of time on this first ship, he was transferred to a T-2 tanker, in which he made several voyages (including one through a powerful hurricane in which it foundered) before being transferred suddenly to the SS *James Harrod*. This would be his last ship.[298]

Returning from its maiden voyage, Hoehling wrote that the SS *James Harrod* had made a splendid record and that the entire crew was proud of the ship's action. No further news of the ship was received until the *Harrodsburg Herald* editor D.M. Hutton received a business letter from Hoehling, head of an aviation news service in Washington, D.C. His letter stated, "Incidentally, you may be interested in the fate of the SS James Harrod, named after the founder of Harrodsburg. I was in command of the gun crew on the ships last voyage. We collided and burned in the North Sea, January 16, 1945. We lost four men."[299]

Unfortunately, while the SS *James Harrod* was en route from New York to Antwerp, Belgium, with barrels of eighty-octane gasoline and army trucks, it was lost in a collision with another American ship. On January 16, 1945, near Deal Castle in Deal, Kent, the SS *James Harrod* collided with the SS

Top: Moving the jerry cans of gasoline off the SS *James Harrod. Deal Library.*

Bottom: Continuation of the gasoline removal from the SS *James Harrod. Deal Library.*

Reymond B. Stevens. Upon collision, the SS *James Harrod* exploded and burned and was beached off Kingsdown in Pegwell Bay by tugboats. Several days later, it was refloated and driven northward until the SS *James Harrod* grounded on the Malm Rocks in Kent.[300]

In the resulting inferno, some of the *Harrod*'s men escaped in the two remaining lifeboats, while a few, Hoehling included, waited on board while gasoline tins exploded like shells. Four of the gun crew were killed. As the men of the SS *James Harrod* worked to control the flames, a Dutch fishing trawler, the *Tromp*, came upon the burning ship. The captain, Bill Mulders, worried about tangling the cargo nets, but he swept through the outer flames and pulled up alongside the *Harrod*. "Yump! Fast, now…yump!" (According to Hoehling, this was the captain's pronunciation of "jump.") There was a fifteen-foot drop down to the slippery deck from the *Harrod*.[301]

When Hoehling spoke with the captain, Mulders stated, "We were anchored for the night up the coast. We run mail from Dover to Ostend. My watch reported a ship on fire. I said we better see if someone is alive. We got up anchor." The Dutch crew poured first cocoa then gin for the ship survivors.[302]

Just before dawn the following morning, Mulders upped anchor and headed for shore. As he did, a fireboat appeared beside the flaming wreck of the *Harrod* and began to spray water astern. When the *Tromp* reached shore, the survivors were taken to a local naval hospital. Most men were suffering from hypothermia, and nurses worked through the morning to regulate their temperatures.[303]

These are the four men who lost their lives on the SS *James Harrod*:

- *Graydon Edward Taylor, Gunners Mate 3rd class, age 22 from Everett, Boston—repatriated. At rest at Greenwood Cemetery.*
- *Walter T. Porter, Seaman First Class, from South Natick, Massachusetts. He is buried in the Americans Cemetery, Cambridge, UK.*
- *James F. Ricketts, First Class from Homer, Louisiana, son of Mary Lou. James was the third son of Mary who was lost in war. James is recorded as Missing in Action.*
- *Paul R. Thompson, Seaman First Class. From Greensboro, North Carolina. Recorded as Missing in Action.*[304]

The SS *James Harrod* broke apart, but much of its cargo from the forward holds was salvaged despite the fire. Fortunately, the wreck lay almost opposite one of four large concrete ramps that had been constructed along the shore at Deal and Walmer to facilitate supply to the military forces around Deal.

This page: The SS *James Harrod* on fire. *Deal Library*.

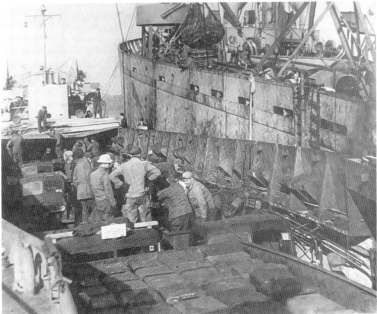

Top: Salvaging operations of the SS *James Harrod*. *Deal Library*.

Bottom: Continued salvage operations on the SS *James Harrod*. *Deal Library*.

Top: These are the four men who lost their lives on the SS *James Harrod*. *Carly Morris.*

Left: The African American men of the 306th Company of the 509th Port Battalion who lost their lives during the salvage of the SS *James Harrod*. *Deal Library.*

Right: The memorial marker for the SS *James Harrod* at Kingsdown beach in Deal, Kent. *Carly Morris.*

The ramp closest to the *James Harrod*, which lay opposite Cambridge Road, proved an ideal staging point for salvaging.

The African American men of the 306th Company of the 509th Port Battalion arrived to undertake the next stage of the salvage operation. Unfortunately, during the salvage of the gasoline jerrycans, disaster struck. One of the gas tankers was being filled when a spark, possibly from a cigarette, ignited the gas vapor in the air from the cans, and there was an explosion. The 250-gallon tanker had been almost full, and the explosion hurled the men from the wagon and killed four men instantly. These men were:

- Harold Beckwith, technician fourth class
- Bennie L.D. Chambers, technician fifth class
- Charles Howard Freeman, private
- William Cornell Paden, technician fourth class[305]

The forward section of the SS *James Harrod* was towed to Sheerness in the hope of welding a stern section to it, but the hulk was abandoned on Blythe Sands and nothing else was done. On May 17, 1946, this section was towed to the River Blackwater and then on to Bremerhaven via Antwerp. On June 20, 1947, it was taken out to sea, packed with three thousand tons of chemical ammunition and scuttled in 2,200 feet of water.

The blackened stern section remained at Walmer for a few years and became a tourist curiosity, mostly being used as a diving platform for local youths. The wreck was finally demolished by a helmeted diver named Larry Parks. Eyewitness Keith Shorten recalled the event:

I joined the Walmer Sea Scout cubs in 1948 and was rowed around the wreck to have a look. On the seaward side you could look into the broken off decks and see the remains of burnt-out jeeps and trucks About then the wreck started to be salvaged by one man operating on his own. Sitting on the beach us kids watched him working over a couple of summers. All he had was an oxy-acetylene flame cutter and a sledgehammer. Starting at the top he nibbled away at the ship structure cutting off manageable sized bits of steel plate, bring them ashore and piling them on the beach for collection. I used to watch from the shore fascinated as he swung the sledgehammer over his head to knock off bits of plate. He was far enough away for the sound to be delayed so that the "boing!" was heard as he swung the hammer high over his head for the next blow. That was my first clue that the speed of light is much faster than the speed of sound.[306]

On January 16, 2020, on the seventy-fifth anniversary, Les Langley, an armed forces veteran and chainsaw carver, erected a pillar monument to the SS *James Harrod* at Kingsdown beach adjacent to the Zetland Arms public house to remember the four men killed on the ship. The memorial plaque to the fallen at Walmer Station was unveiled on September 12, 2021, being delayed by a year due to COVID-19 restrictions.[307]

To this day, a few scraps remain of the ship on the seabed, occasionally visited by divers and providing a welcome shelter to lobsters and other sealife.

THE JAMES HARROD GAVEL

While researching James Harrod's life for this book, I came upon an unusual newspaper article in the local *Harrodsburg Herald*. It talks about a gavel used by James Harrod and given to Kentucky Speaker of the House Julian Carroll. According to a newspaper article, on February 1, 1968:

> *Kentucky House Speaker Julian Carroll, a Democrat from west Paducah, called the House to order with an historic gavel. The five-pound wooden gavel was presented to Carroll during a late January night's session by Representative I.C. James, a Democrat from Harrodsburg. "No one wants the speaker to command the attention of the House more than me or the people in Harrodsburg," James said. "So, we are giving him probably the oldest gavel in the country."*
>
> *James explained the gavel was first used by James Harrod in 1774 and besides keeping the town council in order also helped to "quiet a few Indians now and then." Carroll who has displayed a flair for breaking gavels since the Legislature began in early January, said, "This is just what I need. We shouldn't have any more trouble."*[308]

I contacted the dedicated staff at the Harrodsburg Historical Society (HHS) about the gavel. They found an article stating that the gavel was originally given to the HHS by a man named Fred Hardwick around 1935. Using this information, I discovered a *Lexington Herald* article showing that the Masonic Lodge of Louisville made and donated the gavel to James Isenberg of the HHS in 1935 in honor of James Harrod. This gavel was made of wood from the cedars of Lebanon. According to the *Draper Manuscripts*, Harrod did use a gavel at Old Fort Harrod, but there is no

A photo of James Harrod gavel at the Kentucky Capitol at Frankfort before returning to Harrodsburg. *Donna Robinson Holiday.*

mention of wood used or gavel size. This gavel was then presented to Speaker Carroll in 1968.[309]

In 2021, this gavel was returned to the City of Harrodsburg by Julian Carroll, to be used for the upcoming sestercentennial in 2024. It is currently at the Harrodsburg Historical Society, along with a Senate Citation of Julian Carrol giving the gavel back to Harrodsburg.

JAMES HARROD TRUST

The James Harrod Trust is a nonprofit advocate for historical preservation that strives to protect, encourage and continue the preservation of cultural and historic places in Mercer County in order to enhance the quality of life for this and future generations. When the James Harrod Trust was still a dream, it was a small group dedicated to preservation, and they started meeting and making plans, with Helen Dedman serving as the first chairman. When the James Harrod Trust was chartered, it became a group of like-minded preservationists.

The group's mission was the preservation of our historic buildings and sites in order to provide a memorial to those great artisans, craftsmen and architects who planned, developed and built structures made to last. Harrodsburg and Mercer County are fortunate to have structures still standing from the pioneer, antebellum, Victorian and Art Deco eras. Unfortunately, many others have been lost, which is why the James Harrod Trust for Historic Preservation was formed in 1999–2000.

Highlights of the James Harrod Trust include the acquisition and repairs of Dedman Drug Store on Main Street and later the securing of a business/ new owner for the property; the restoration and new ownership of Rocky Point; numerous educational programs, such as rock fence and gravestone cleaning workshops; and events like the Cemetery Tour, Awards Dinners and Porch Tours, as well as the printing of several books.

The organization has formally designated fifty-four James Harrod Trust Historical Markers on properties in the county:

- Fort Harrod
- John McMurtry's Station
- Harrodsburg Baptist Church
- Harrodsburg Christian Church
- United Presbyterian Church
- The Academy
- Old Mercer County Jail
- Morgan Row
- United Methodist Church and Parsonage
- White Hall
- St. Peter African Methodist Episcopal Church
- William McBride House
- Dr. A.D. Price House
- Blue Front Building
- Maria Thomas Daviess House
- Lawyer's Row
- Aspen Hall/Dr. James Shannon House
- Greystone
- Honeysuckle Hill/Fair Oaks
- G.A. Curry House
- Dedman House

The James Harrod Trust Historical Marker for Old Fort Harrod. *Keith Rightmyer.*

- VanArsdall/Sale House
- Poteet House
- Tabler House
- Magoffin/Mills/Gaither House
- Clay Hill
- Lucy Newton Cogar House
- Thompson/Wickliffe House
- Isaac Hipple House
- Muscoe Garnett House
- Hugh McGary House
- Diamond Point
- The Maples
- Rykon
- Forest Pillars
- Dr. James Harrison Moore House
- First Baptist Church/Centennial Baptist Church
- Benjamin Passmore House and Hotel
- Cardwellton
- West Side School
- Mercer County Fair and Horse Show
- Fairview
- Abraham Chapline Plantation/Rufus Henry Vandarsdall House
- Henry Wilson's Station

- Old Mud Meeting House
- Charles Ficklin/Alexander Buchanan House
- Hogue/Williams House
- Courtview
- Tewmey/Armstrong House
- Pulliam/Curry House
- Bataan War Memorial
- John L. Bridges House/Burford Hill
- Spring Hill Cemetery
- Court House Square

JAMES HARROD COIN

For Harrodsburg's 200th anniversary in June 1974, a souvenir coin was minted to commemorate the historic occasion. One side of the coin has a facsimile of James Harrod; unfortunately, he was modeled wearing a coonskin cap. This side also lists the last names of a few men who accompanied Harrod in June 1774. The back side features the James Harrod blockhouse at Old Fort Harrod and states, "Harrodsburg Bicentennial, 1774–1874, The First Settlement of the West."

The front side of the James Harrod coin. *Keith Rightmyer.*

These coins are still available on several auction websites and in local antique stores.

NOTES

Chapter 1

1. Reid, *Daniel Boone and Others*, 46; Schmidt, *Kentucky Illustrated*; Harrison and Klotter, *New History of Kentucky*, 25.
2. Mason, *James Harrod*, 5; Draper, *Life of Daniel Boone*, 555; Leckey, *Tenmile Country*, 240; Withers et al., *Chronicles of Border Warfare*, 190.
3. Leckey, *Tenmile Country*, 241; Draper, *Life of Daniel Boone*, 555; DAR, Fendrick, *American Revolutionary Soldiers of Franklin County*, 96.
4. Kleber et al., *Kentucky Encyclopedia*, 413; Klotter, *History Mysteries*, 11; Mason, *James Harrod*, 10; Leckey, *Tenmile Country*, 247.
5. Groome, *Fauquier during the Proprietorship*, 66.
6. Bain, *Fluorspar Deposits of Southern Illinois*, 177; Draper, *Draper Collection of American*, 37J168-174.
7. Sloan, "Great Cove Massacre"; Withers et al., *Chronicles of Border Warfare*, 190; Draper, *Life of Daniel Boone*, 555; Mason, *James Harrod of Kentucky*, 11.
8. Wonning, *Year of Colonial American History*, 311; Withers et al., *Chronicles of Border Warfare*, 190; Kleber et al., *Kentucky Encyclopedia*, 413.
9. Thornton, *French and Indian War*, 9.
10. Draper, *Life of Daniel Boone*, 555.
11. Middleton, *Pontiac's War*, 109–12; Kleber et al., *Kentucky Encyclopedia*, 413.
12. Tucker et al., *Encyclopedia of the North American Indian Wars*, 360; Kleber, *Encyclopedia of Louisville*, 784; Draper, *Life of Daniel Boone*, 71, 492.

13. Kleber et al., *Kentucky Encyclopedia*, 413; Klotter, *History Mysteries*, 11; Mason, *James Harrod*, 33.

14. Mason, *James Harrod*, 33; Klotter, *History Mysteries*, 11; Kleber et al., *Kentucky Encyclopedia*, 413.

15. Collins, *Collins' Historical Sketches of Kentucky*, 451; Henderson, "Dispelling the Myth," 1–25; Henderson and Pollack, *State-by-State Historical Encyclopedia*, 393–440.

Chapter 2

16. Belue, *Hunters of Kentucky*, 10.
17. Harrison and Klotter, *New History of Kentucky*, 18.
18. Cotterill, *History of Pioneer Kentucky*, Kindle location 491–96.
19. Ibid., Kindle location 496–506.
20. Mason, *James Harrod*, 36.
21. Draper, *Life of Daniel Boone*, 123.
22. Clarke, *Kentucky's Age of Wood*, 7.
23. Catlett, "Kentucky Flintlock Long Rifle."
24. Dillin, *Kentucky Rifle*.
25. Catlett, "Kentucky Flintlock Long Rifle."
26. Mason, *James Harrod*, 37.
27. Draper, *Life of Daniel Boone*, 123.
28. Ibid., 227.
29. Cotterill, *History of Pioneer Kentucky*, Kindle location 961–71.
30. Belue, *Hunters of Kentucky*, 72.
31. Ibid., 73.
32. Draper, *Draper Collection of Americana*, 14J58-84.
33. Mason, *James Harrod*, 38.
34. Collins, *Collins' Historical Sketches of Kentucky*, 55.
35. Draper, *Life of Daniel Boone*, 252.
36. Cotterill, *History of Pioneer Kentucky*, Kindle location 982–92.
37. Thwaites *Documentary History of Dunmore's War*, 68.
38. Mason, *James Harrod*, 41.
39. Thwaites, *Documentary History of Dunmore's War*, 432.
40. Belue, *Hunters of Kentucky*, 78.
41. Harrison and Klotter, *New History of Kentucky*, 19.
42. Abernethy, *Western Lands and the American Revolution*, 98–112.
43. Krull, *What Was the Boston Tea Party?*, 4–5.

Chapter 3

44. Downes, *Council Fires on the Upper Ohio*, 152.

45. Elliott, *Long Hunter*, 75.

46. Mason, *James Harrod*, 243.

47. Collins, *Collins' Historical Sketches of Kentucky*, 517.

48. *Automobile Blue Book*, 4:423.

49. Kleber et al., *Kentucky Encyclopedia*, 414.

50. From the booklet "Fort Harrod."

51. Cotterill, *History of Pioneer Kentucky*, Kindle location 1,029–41.

52. Mason, *James Harrod*, 244.

53. Clark, *Voice of the Frontier*, 10.

54. Mason, *James Harrod*, 244.

55. Ibid., 47.

56. Collins, *Collins' Historical Sketches of Kentucky*, 518.

57. Ibid., 517.

58. Clark, *History of Kentucky*, 13, 36.

59. *Harrodsburg Herald*, January 12, 1995.

60. Caruso, *Appalachian Frontier*, Kindle location 2,069–79.

61. Elliott, *Long Hunter*, 76.

62. Cotterill, *History of Pioneer Kentucky*, Kindle location 1,088–99.

63. Kellogg, "Kentucky Pioneer Tells Her Story."

64. Cotterill, *History of Pioneer Kentucky*, Kindle location 1,041–45.

65. Mason, *James Harrod*, 62.

66. Cotterill, *History of Pioneer Kentucky*, Kindle location 1,110–15.

67. Eckert, *Sorrow on Our Heart*, 103.

68. Draper, *Draper Collection of Americana*, 27CC33.

69. McAfee, "Life and Times of Robert B. McAfee," 23.

70. Mercer Online, "History," http://www.merceronline.com/history.htm.

Chapter 4

71. Kleber et al., *Kentucky Encyclopedia*, 344.

72. Harrison and Klotter, *New History of Kentucky*, 24.

73. Cotterill, *History of Pioneer Kentucky*, Kindle location 944–51.

74. Harrison, *George Rogers Clark and the War in the West*, chapter 1.

75. Clark, *History of Kentucky*, 43–45.

76. Fenge and Aldridge, *Keeping Promises*, xvii.

77. Lester, *Transylvania Company*, 29–47.
78. Harrison and Klotter, *New History of Kentucky*, 27.
79. Cotterill, *History of Pioneer Kentucky*, Kindle location 1,448–60.
80. Mercer Online, "History."
81. Cotterill, *History of Pioneer Kentucky*, Kindle location 1,436–43.
82. Caruso, *Appalachian Frontier*, Kindle location 2,492–2,515.
83. Draper, *Draper Collection of Americana*, 1CC21-102.
84. Hammon and Taylor, *Virginia's Western War*, 13–14.
85. Draper, *Draper Collection of Americana*, 1CC21-102.
86. Collins, *Collins' Historical Sketches of Kentucky*, 499–500.
87. Mercer Online, "History."
88. Belue, *Long Hunt*, 109.
89. Cotterill, *History of Pioneer Kentucky*, Kindle location 1,460–83.
90. Collins, *Collins' Historical Sketches of Kentucky*, 500.
91. Harrison and Klotter, *New History of Kentucky*, 29.
92. Perrin et al., *Kentucky*, 134.
93. Saunders, *Colonial Records of North Carolina*, 1,267–69.
94. Henderson, *Richard Henderson and the Occupation of Kentucky*, 341–63.
95. Collins, *Collins' Historical Sketches of Kentucky*, 501–8.
96. Cotterill, *History of Pioneer Kentucky*, Kindle location 1,489–1,520.
97. Belue, *Long Hunt*, 108.
98. Hall, *Sketches of the History*, 266–67.
99. Hammon and Taylor, *Virginia's Western War*, 19–20.
100. Cotterill, *History of Pioneer Kentucky*, Kindle location 1,552–63.
101. Caruso, *Appalachian Frontier*, Kindle location 2,795–96.
102. Cotterill, *History of Pioneer Kentucky*, Kindle location 1,568–89.
103. Lester, *Transylvania Colony*, 127–29.
104. Draper, *Life of Daniel Boone*, 403.
105. Butler, *History of the Commonwealth of Kentucky*, 28–29.
106. Kleber et al., *Kentucky Encyclopedia*, 344.
107. Draper, *Draper Collection of Americana*, 12CC65.
108. Armstrong, *Harrodsburg and Mercer County*, 20–21.
109. Friend, *Buzzel About Kentuck*, 66.
110. Kornwolf, *Architecture and Town Planning*, 1,477.
111. Draper, *Life of Daniel Boone*, 182.
112. Mercer Online, "History."
113. Mason, *James Harrod*, 89.
114. Zenzen, *Fort Stanwix National Monument*, 17.
115. Trabue, *Westward into Kentucky*, 48.

116. Harrison, *George Rogers Clark and the War in the West*, chapter 1.
117. Draper, *Life of Daniel Boone*, 426.

Chapter 5

118. Ibid., 424.
119. Harrison and Klotter, *New History of Kentucky*, 33.
120. Lawrence, *Colonial Families of America*, 316–22.
121. Draper, *Life of Daniel Boone*, 403.
122. Ibid., 252.
123. Ibid., 405.
124. Ibid., 409.
125. *Harrodsburg Herald*, January 12, 1995.
126. Draper, *Life of Daniel Boone*, 406–7.
127. Ibid., 424.
128. Mason, *James Harrod*, 91.
129. Hammon and Taylor, *Virginia's Western War*, 33.
130. Caruso, *Appalachian Frontier*, Kindle locations 2,850–51.
131. Draper, *Life of Daniel Boone*, 409–10.
132. Draper, *Draper Collection of Americana*, 14S2.
133. Robertson, *Petitions of the Early Inhabitants of Kentucky*, 36–38.
134. Cotterill, *History of Pioneer Kentucky*, Kindle location 1,632–81.
135. Clark, *George Rogers Clark Papers*, 15.
136. Harrison and Klotter, *New History of Kentucky*, 34.
137. Draper, *Life of Daniel Boone*, 493.
138. Harrison, *George Rogers Clark*, 9.
139. Waddell, *Annuals of Augusta County*.
140. Harrison, *George Rogers Clark*, 9–10.
141. Draper, *Life of Daniel Boone*, 447.
142. Caruso, *Appalachian Frontier*, Kindle location 2,931–62.
143. Cotterill, *History of Pioneer Kentucky*, Kindle location 1,702–27.
144. Clark, *Voice of the Frontier*, 14.
145. Nester, "I Glory in War," 48.
146. Hammon and Taylor, *Virginia's Western War*, 49.
147. Harrison and Klotter, *New History of Kentucky*, 32.

Chapter 6

148. Belue, *Hunters of Kentucky*, 119.
149. Withers et al., *Chronicles of Border Warfare*, 200.
150. Elliott, *Long Hunter*, 110.
151. Draper, *Life of Daniel Boone*, 435.
152. Ibid., 438.
153. Cotterill, *History of Pioneer Kentucky*, Kindle location 1,801–16.
154. Ibid., Kindle location 1,816–27.
155. Friend, *Buzzel About Kentuck*, 63.
156. Draper, *Draper Collection of Americana*, 48J10-12, 4CC30-36.
157. Harrison and Klotter, *New History of Kentucky*, 35.
158. Draper, *Life of Daniel Boone*, 439.
159. Ibid., 162–63.
160. Hammon and Taylor, *Virginia's Western War*, 55–56.
161. Clark, *Voice of the Frontier*, 14.
162. Draper, *Life of Daniel Boone*, 439.
163. Hammon and Taylor, *Virginia's Western War*, 56.
164. Draper, *Life of Daniel Boone*, 442.
165. Ibid.
166. Ibid., 443.
167. Draper, *Draper Collection of Americana*, 12C26-29.
168. Ibid., 26CC55, 4CC30.
169. Harrison and Klotter, *New History of Kentucky*, 34.
170. Draper, *Life of Daniel Boone*, 446.
171. Kellogg, "Kentucky Pioneer Tells Her Story."
172. Draper, *Life of Daniel Boone*, 447.
173. Johnston, *Famous Frontiersmen and Heroes of the Border*, 8.
174. Draper, *Life of Daniel Boone*, 447.
175. The corncrib skirmish took place on September 22, 1777; Eli Gerrard was one of the men killed on this occasion.
176. Draper, *Life of Daniel Boone*, 457.
177. Belue, *Hunters of Kentucky*, 143.
178. Clark, *George Rogers Clark Papers*.
179. Klotter, *History Mysteries*, 22–24.
180. Smyth, *Tour in the United States of America*.
181. Lawrence, *Colonial Families of America*, 316–22.
182. Marshal, *History of Kentucky*.
183. Young, *Westward into Kentucky*, 168.

184. Draper, *Life of Daniel Boone*, 449–50.
185. Ibid., 451.

Chapter 7

186. Draper, *Draper Collection of Americana*, 17CC192, 12CC45, 12CC112.
187. Doddridge, *Notes on the Settlement and Indian Wars*.
188. Hendrickson, *Early American Dance Music Collection*.
189. Doddridge, *Notes on the Settlement and Indian Wars*.
190. Farr, *My Appalachia*, 101.
191. Mason, *James Harrod of Kentucky*, 53.
192. Collins, *Collins' Historical Sketches of Kentucky*, vol. 2.
193. Henkle, "Obituary of Ann Harrod."
194. Kleber et al., *Kentucky Encyclopedia*, 195.
195. Belue, *Hunters of Kentucky*, 147.
196. Kellogg, "Kentucky Pioneer Tells Her Story."
197. Clark, "Salt, a Factor in the Settlement of Kentucky," 42–45.
198. Draper, *Life of Daniel Boone*, 489.
199. Lester, *Transylvania Colony*.
200. Virginia General Assembly Senate, *Journal of the Senate of Virginia*.

Chapter 8

201. Draper, *Life of Daniel Boone*, 574.
202. Kincaid and Monaghan, *Wilderness Road*.
203. Marshall, *History of Kentucky*, 98.
204. Bibb, *Reports of Cases at Common Law and in Chancery*.
205. Marshall, *History of Kentucky*.
206. Draper, *Draper Collection of Americana*, 17J6.
207. Kentucky Historical Society, "Certificate Book of the Virginia Land Commissioners," 11–12.
208. Ibid., *Register of the Kentucky Historical Society*, 5–7.
209. Stephenson, "Historic Homes of Harrodsburg, Kentucky," 7, 9–14.
210. Klotter, *History Mysteries*, 17.
211. Mereness, "Journal of Colonel William Fleming," 622–30.
212. Ibid., 630.
213. Draper, *Draper Collection of Americana*, 12C23.

214. Leckey, *Tenmile Country*, 241.

215. Mason, *James Harrod*, 181.

216. Talbert, "Kentucky Invades Ohio," 291–300.

217. Tucker, *Almanac of American Military History*, 1:340.

218. Clark, *George Rogers Clark Papers*.

219. Draper, *Draper Collection of Americana*, 17CC24.

220. Clark, *George Rogers Clark Papers*, 404–6.

221. Kellogg, "Kentucky Pioneer Tells Her Story."

222. See Bodley, *History of Kentucky Before the Louisiana Purchase in 1803*.

223. Mason, *James Harrod*, 183.

224. "Memorials from Illinois, Kentucky 1780–1788."

225. Draper, *Draper Collection of Americana*, 28CC61.

226. Clark, *George Rogers Clark Papers*.

227. Palmer, "Virginia State Papers II," *Calendar of Virginia State Papers and Other Manuscripts* (1893), 313–15.

228. Butler, *History of the Commonwealth of Kentucky*, 117.

229. Mason, *James Harrod of Kentucky*, 187.

230. Draper, *Draper Collection of Americana*, 9J21.

231. Ibid., 11CC54-66.

232. Mason, *James Harrod of Kentucky*.

233. Draper, *Draper Collection of Americana*, 9J21.

234. Clark, *George Rogers Clark*, 451–84.

Chapter 9

235. Perrin, *Counties of Christian and Trigg, Kentucky*, 46.

236. Palmer, *Calendar of Virginia State Papers and Other Manuscripts*, 21–23.

237. Marshal, *History of Kentucky*, 122.

238. Stephenson, "Old Courthouse and the Courts and Bar of Mercer County."

239. Draper, *Draper Collection of Americana*, 12C24.

240. Marshal, *History of Kentucky*, 114–18.

241. Kellogg, "Kentucky Pioneer Tells Her Story."

242. Ibid.

243. Clark, *George Rogers Clark Papers*, 89–109.

244. Belue, *Hunters of Kentucky*, 179.

245. Draper, *Draper Collection of Americana*, 12CC50.

246. Thorn and Thorn, *Warrior Women*, 451.

247. Belue, *Hunters of Kentucky*, 179.
248. Mason, *James Harrod*, 202–3.

Chapter 10

249. Ibid., 204.
250. Stephenson, "Some Early Industries of Mercer County," 43–52.
251. Lee et al., *Water in Kentucky*, 27.
252. Clark, *George Rogers Clark Papers*, 6–11.
253. Stephenson, "Old Courthouse and the Courts and Bar of Mercer County."
254. Butler, *History of the Commonwealth of Kentucky*, 143.
255. Mason, *James Harrod*, 208.
256. Abernethy, "First Kentucky Convention," in *Western Lands*, 67.
257. Ibid., 67–68.
258. Ibid., 297–300.
259. Robertson, *Petitions of the Early Inhabitants of Kentucky*, 82.
260. Littell, *Statute Law of Kentucky*, 552.

Chapter 11

261. Imlay, *Topographical Description of the Western Territory*, 136.
262. Collins, *Collins' Historical Sketches of Kentucky*, 20.
263. Kleber, *Encyclopedia of Louisville*, 361.
264. Mercer County Probate Office, "Inventory of James Harrod's Estate," 146–49.
265. Dillin, *Kentucky Rifle*, 13.
266. Mason, *James Harrod*, 215.
267. Draper, *Draper Collection of Americana*, 12CC112.
268. Ibid.
269. Mason, *James Harrod*, 219.
270. Draper, *Draper Collection of Americana*, 12C25.
271. Jillson, "Old Kentucky Entries and Deeds," 38, 217, 419, 498, 562.
272. Mason, *James Harrod*, 221–22.
273. Mercer County Order Books, Office of the Clerk, *Docket Book of Circuit Court* (Packet D, I, Harrodsburg), and Lincoln County Order Book I (Stanford).

274. Monroe, *Reports of Cases at Common Law*, 136–41.
275. Harrison and Klotter, *New History of Kentucky*, 53.
276. Kleber et al., *Kentucky Encyclopedia*, 849.
277. Ibid., 852.
278. Thorpe, *Federal and State Constitutions*, 3:1,264.

Chapter 12

279. Mason, *James Harrod*, 207–8.
280. Palmer, *Calendar of Virginia State Papers and Other Manuscripts*, 258–60.
281. Klotter, *History Mysteries*, 24.
282. Mason, *James Harrod*, 230.
283. Ibid., 230.
284. Coulter, "Early Frontier Democracy in the First Kentucky Constitution," 665–77.
285. Shaler, *Kentucky*, 122.
286. Mason, *James Harrod*, 68.
287. Steely, *Swift's Silver Mines*, 22.
288. Mason, *James Harrod*, 70.
289. "Mercer County Will Book I" (1792), 15.
290. Mason, *James Harrod*, 32.
291. Old Fort Harrod State Park, *Pioneer Cemetery Marker*.
292. "Mercer County Marriage Register I" (1794), 96.
293. Littell, *Statute Law of Kentucky III*, 196.
294. Jillson, "Founding of Harrodsburg," 559–62.
295. Ibid., 559–62.
296. Redford, *From the Conference 1820 to the Conference 1832*.

Appendix

297. *Harrodsburg Herald*, June 25, 1948.
298. Hoehling, *Fighting Liberty Ships*, 119.
299. *Harrodsburg Herald*, June 25, 1948.
300. Heritage Gateway, "Historic England Research Records."
301. Hoehling, *Fighting Liberty Ships*, 133.
302. Ibid.
303. Ibid., 135.

304. Eyden, *Walmer Station Memorial*, 25.
305. Ibid., 26.
306. Ibid., 24.
307. Ibid.
308. *Harrodsburg Herald*, February 1, 1968.
309. *Lexington Herald*, November 3, 1935.

BIBLIOGRAPHY

Abernethy, Thomas Perkins. *Western Lands and the American Revolution*. New York: Russell and Russell, 1937.

Armstrong, Anna. *Harrodsburg and Mercer County*. Charlottesville, SC: Arcadia Publishing, 2013.

Automobile Blue Book. Vol. 4, *Ohio, Native Americana, Michigan, Kentucky*. N.p.: Automobile Blue Book Publishing Company, 1917.

Bain, H. Foster. *The Fluorspar Deposits of Southern Illinois*. Washington, D.C.: U.S. Government Printing Office, 1905.

Belue, Ted Franklin. *The Hunters of Kentucky: A Narrative History of America's First Far West, 1750–1790*. Mechanicsburg, PA: Stackpole Books, 2011.

———. *The Long Hunt: Death of the Buffalo East of the Mississippi*. Mechanicsburg, PA: Stackpole Books, 1996.

Bibb, George M. *Reports of Cases at Common Law and in Chancery, Argued and Decided in the Court of Appeals of the Commonwealth of Kentucky*. Williamsburg, VA: George M. Bibb, 1815.

Bodley, Temple. *History of Kentucky Before the Louisiana Purchase in 1803*. Chicago: S.J. Clarke Publishing Company, 1928.

Butler, Mann. *A History of the Commonwealth of Kentucky*. Carlisle, KY: Applewood Books, 2010.

Caruso, John A. *The Appalachian Frontier: America's First Surge*. Knoxville: University of Tennessee Press, 1959.

Catlett, Larry. "Kentucky Flintlock Long Rifle." Friends of the Fort. http://friendsoffortharrod.com/story-of-old-fort-harrod.htm.

Clark, George Rogers. *George Rogers Clark Papers, 1771–1781*. Trustees of the Illinois State Historical Library, 1912.

Clark, Thomas D. *A History of Kentucky*. Lexington, KY: John Bradford Press, 1950.

———. "Salt, a Factor in the Settlement of Kentucky." *Filson Club History Quarterly* (1958).

———. *The Voice of the Frontier: John Bradford's Notes on Kentucky*. Lexington: University Press of Kentucky, 2015.

Clarke, Kenneth. *Kentucky's Age of Wood*. Lexington: University of Press of Kentucky, 1976.

Collins, Lewis. *Collins' Historical Sketches of Kentucky: History of Kentucky*. Vol. 2. Covington, KY: Collins and Company, 1882.

Cotterill, Robert Spencer. *The History of Pioneer Kentucky*. Cincinnati: Johnson and Hardin, 1917.

Coulter, E. Merton. "Early Frontier Democracy in the First Kentucky Constitution." *Political Science Quarterly* (1924).

Dillin, John Grace Wolfe. *The Kentucky Rifle: A Study of the Origin and Development of a Purely American Type of Firearm*. Whitefish, MT: Literary Licensing, LLC, 2011.

Doddridge, Joseph. *Notes on the Settlement and Indian Wars*. London: John Ritenour and William Lindsey, 1912.

Downes, Randolph C. *Council Fires on the Upper Ohio: A Narrative of Native American Affairs in the Upper Ohio Valley Until 1795*. Pittsburgh, PA: University of Pittsburgh Press, 2014.

Draper, Lyman Copeland. *Draper Collection of Americana*. Madison, Wisconsin Historical Society, 17CC24, 1CC21-102, 4CC30, 9J21, 12C25, 11CC54-66, 12CC112, 12CC23, 12CC24, 12CC45, 12CC50, 17CC192, 17J6, 26CC55, 27CC33, 28CC61, 37J168-174 and 48J10-12.

———. "John Shane Interviews." *Draper Collection of Americana*. Madison: Wisconsin Historical Society, 12CC65.

———. *The Life of Daniel Boone*. Mechanicsburg, PA: Stackpole Books, 1998.

———. "Thomas Hanson Journal." *Draper Collection of Americana*. Madison: Wisconsin Historical Society, 14J58-84.

East Kent Maritime Trust. Kent, UK: Bath Royal Literary, July 23, 1984.

Eckert, Allan W. *A Sorrow in Our Heart: The Life of Tecumseh*. New York: Bantam, 1993.

Elliott, Lawrence. *The Long Hunter*. Virginia: Allen & Unwin, 1977.

Eyden, Phil. *The Walmer Station Memorial*. London: Walmer Parish Council, 2021.

Farr, Sidney Saylor. *My Appalachia: A Memoir*. Lexington: University Press of Kentucky, 2014.

Fendrick, Virginia Shannon, DAR. *American Revolutionary Soldiers of Franklin County, Pennsylvania*. Chambersburg, PA: Franklin County Chapter Daughters of the American Revolution, 1944.

Fenge, Terry, and Jim Aldridge. *Keeping Promises: The Royal Proclamation of 1763, Aboriginal Rights, and Treaties in Canada*. Quebec, CAN: McGill-Queen's University Press, 2015.

The Filson Club. "Lyman C. Draper Sketch of James Harrod." *Filson Club History Quarterly* 32 (1958).

Frank, Andrew K. *Early Republic: People and Perspectives*. Santa Barbara, CA: ABC-CLIO, 2008.

Friend, Craig Thompson. *The Buzzel About Kentuck: Settling the Promised Land*. Lexington: University Press of Kentucky, 1999.

Groome, Harry Connolly. *Fauquier during the Proprietorship*. Richmond, VA: Clearfield Publishing, 1927.

Hall, James. *Sketches of the History, Life, and Manners of the West*. Vol. 2. Philadelphia, PA: Harrison Hall, 1835.

Hammon, Neal O., and Richard Taylor. *Virginia's Western War: 1775–1786*. Mechanicsburg, PA: Stackpole Books, 2002.

Harrison, Lowell H. *George Rogers Clark and the War in the West*. Lexington: University Press of Kentucky, 2014.

Harrison, Lowell H., and James C. Klotter. *A New History of Kentucky*. Lexington: University Press of Kentucky, 1997.

Harrodsburg Herald. 1927.

———. June 25, 1948.

Henderson, A. Gwynn. "Dispelling the Myth: Seventeenth- and Eighteenth-Century Indian Life in Kentucky." *Register of the Kentucky Historical Society* 90, no. 1 (1992): 1–25.

Henderson, A. Gwynn, and David Pollack. "Kentucky." In *Native America: A State-by-State Historical Encyclopedia*. Vol. 1, *Alabama-Louisiana*. Edited by Daniel Murphree. Santa Barbara, CA: Greenwood, 2012.

Henderson, Archibald. *Richard Henderson and the Occupation of Kentucky, 1775*. Cedar Rapids, MI: Mississippi Valley Historical Review, 1915.

Hendrickson, Charles C., and Frances C. Hendrickson. *Early American Dance Music Collection*. N.p.: Hendrickson Group, 1788.

Henkle, M.M. "Obituary of Ann Harrod." *Western Christian Advocate*, May 12, 1843.

Heritage Gateway. "Historic England Research Records: James Harrod." http://www.pastscape.org.uk/hob.aspx?hob_id=904394.

Hoehling, A.A. *The Fighting Liberty Ships: A Memoir*. First American Edition. Kent, UK: Kent State University, 1990.

Imlay, Gilbert. *A Topographical Description of the Western Territory of North America*. Dublin: William James, 1793.

Jillson, Willard R. "The Founding of Harrodsburg." *Register of Kentucky State Historical Society*, no. 81 (1929).

———. "Old Kentucky Entries and Deeds." *Filson Club Publication* 34 (1926).

Johnston, Charles H.L. *Famous Frontiersmen and Heroes of the Border: Famous Leders Series*. Boston: L.C. Page & Company, 1913.

Kellogg, Louise Phelps. *Frontier Retreat on the Upper Ohio, 1779–1781*. Madison: State Historical Society of Wisconsin, 1917.

———. "A Kentucky Pioneer Tells Her Story of Early Boonesborough and Harrodsburg." *History Quarterly of the Filson Club* 3, no. 5 (1929).

Kentucky Historical Society. "Certificate Book of the Virginia Land Commissioners." *Register of the Kentucky Historical Society*. Frankfort, 1923.

Kincaid, Robert L., and Jay Monaghan. *The Wilderness Road*. Whitefish, MT: Literary Licensing, 2013.

Kleber, John E. *The Encyclopedia of Louisville*. Lexington: University Press of Kentucky, 2000.

Kleber, John E., Thomas D. Clark, Lowell H. Harrison and James C. Klotter. *The Kentucky Encyclopedia*. Lexington: University Press of Kentucky, 2015.

Klotter, James C. *The Breckinridges of Kentucky*. Lexington: University Press of Kentucky, 2015.

———. *History Mysteries*. Lexington: University Press of Kentucky, 1989.

Kornwolf, James D. *Architecture and Town Planning in Colonial North America*. Vol. 1. Baltimore, MD: John Hopkins University Press, 2003.

Krull, Kathleen. *What Was the Boston Tea Party?* New York: Grosset and Dunlap, 2013.

Lawrence, Ruth, ed. *Colonial Families of America*. Vol. 3. New York: National Americana Society, 1931.

Leckey, Howard L. *The Tenmile Country and Its Pioneer Families*. Baltimore, MD: Genealogical Publishing Company, 2009.

Lee, Brian D., Daniel I. Carey and Alice L. Jones. *Water in Kentucky: Natural History, Communities, and Conservation*. Lexington: University Press of Kentucky, 2017.

Lester, William Stewart. *The Transylvania Company*. Lexington, KY: S.R. Guard and Company, 1935.

Lincoln County Order Book, Office of the Clerk. *Docket Book of Circuit Court.* Stanford, Packet I. Stanford.

Littell, William. *Statute Law of Kentucky.* Virginia: William Hunter Press, 1810.

Marshal, Humphrey. *History of Kentucky.* Frankfort, KY: George S. Robinson, 1824.

McAfee, Robert Breckinridge. "The Life and Times of Robert B. McAfee and His Family Connections." *Register of the Kentucky State Historical Society* 25 (1927).

"Memorials from Illinois, Kentucky 1780–1788." *Papers of the Continental Congress*, vol. 48. Library of Congress, 1788.

Mercer County Order Books, Office of the Clerk. *Docket Book of Circuit Court.* Harrodsburg, KY, Packet D, I, Harrodsburg.

Mercer County Probate Office. "Inventory of James Harrod's Estate." Mercer County Will Book I, February 1794.

Mereness, Newton D. "Journal of Colonel William Fleming." *Mereness's Travels in the American Colonies, 1779–1780.* New York: McMillian Company, 1916.

Middleton, Richard. *Pontiac's War: Its Causes, Course and Consequences.* Abingdon, Oxfordshire: Taylor and Franklin, 2012.

Monroe, Thomas Benjamin. *Reports of Cases at Common Law and in Equity Decided in the Court of Appeals of Kentucky.* Vol. 5. Cincinnati, 1909.

Nester, William. "I Glory in War." *George Rogers Clark.* Norman: University of Oklahoma Press, 2012.

Old Fort Harrod State Park. *Pioneer Cemetery Marker.* Harrodsburg.

Palmer, William Pitt. "Virginia State Papers IV." *Calendar of Virginia State Papers and Other Manuscripts.* Richmond, VA: H.W. Flournoy, 1893.

Perrin, William H., J.H. Battle, G.C. Kniffin and G.S. Kniffin. *Kentucky: A History of the State.* Columbia, KY: F.A. Battey, 1887.

Perrin, William Henry. *Counties of Christian and Trigg, Kentucky: Historical and Biographical.* Louisville, KY: F.A. Battey, 1884.

Redford, Albert Henry. *From the Conference 1820 to the Conference 1832.* Nashville, TN: Southern Methodist Publishing, 1870.

Reid, Darren R. *Daniel Boone and Others on the Kentucky Frontier.* Jefferson, NC: McFarland, 2009.

———. *Daniel Boone and Others on the Kentucky Frontier: Autobiographies and Narratives, 1769–1795.* Jefferson, NC: McFarland, 2009.

Robertson, James Rood. *Petitions of the Early Inhabitants of Kentucky to the General Assembly of Virginia, 1769–1792.* Louisville, KY: John P. Morton Inc., printers to the Filson Club, 1910.

Saunders, William Laurence. *The Colonial Records of North Carolina,* IX. Raleigh, NC: P.M. Hale State Printer, 1890.

Schmidt, Martin F. *Kentucky Illustrated: The First Hundred Years.* Lexington: University of Kentucky Press, 2014.

Shaler, Nathaniel Southgate. *Kentucky, a Pioneer Commonwealth.* Boston: Houghton Mifflin, 1912.

Sloan, Walter Reed. "Great Cove Massacre—Fulton County, Pennsylvania—1 November 1755." *Sloan-Trout, Tom and Tillie's Ancestors.* Madison: University of Wisconsin, 2007.

Smyth, John F.D. *Tour in the United States of America.* London: G. Robinson, 1784.

Steely, Michael S. *Swift's Silver Mines and Related Appalachian Treasures.* Johnson City, TN: Overmountain Press, 1995.

Stephenson, Mary A. "Some Early Industries of Mercer County." *Register of Kentucky State Historical Society* 13, no. 38 (1915).

Stephenson, W.W. *A Pamphlet of Historic Facts and a Description of the Old Fort and the Present Replica.* Harrodsburg, KY: Harrodsburg Herald, 1931.

Stephenson, William Worth. "Historic Homes of Harrodsburg, Kentucky." *Register of Kentucky State Historical Society* 10, no. 30 (1912).

———. "The Old Courthouse and the Courts and Bar of Mercer County." *Register of the Kentucky Historical Society*, no. 7 (1909).

Talbert, Charles G. "Kentucky Invades Ohio—1780." *Register of the Kentucky State Historical Society* 52, no. 181 (1954).

Thorn, James Alexander, and Dark Rain Thorn. *Warrior Women: The Exceptional Life Story of Nonhelema, Shawnee Indian Woman Chief.* New York: Random House Publishing Group, 2007.

Thornton, Jeremy. *The French and Indian War.* New York: Rosen Publishing Group, 2002.

Thorpe, Frances N. *The Federal and State Constitutions.* Vol. 3. Vermont: U.S. Government Printing Office, 1909.

Thwaites, Reuben Gold, and Kellogg Louise Phelps. *Documentary History of Dunmore's War.* Madison: Wisconsin Historical Society, 1905.

Trabue, Daniel. *Westward into Kentucky: The Memoirs of Daniel Trabue.* Edited by Chester Raymond Young. Lexington: University Press of Kentucky, 1981.

Tucker, Spencer. *Almanac of American Military History.* Vol. 1. Santa Barbara, CA: ABC-CLIO Publishing City, 2013.

Tucker, Spencer, James Arnold and Roberta Wiener. *The Encyclopedia of the North American Indian Wars, 1607–1890: A Political, Social, and Military History.* Santa Barbara, CA: ABC-CLIO, 2011.

Virginia General Assembly Senate. *Journal of the Senate of Virginia*. Williamsburg: Virginia General Assembly Senate, 1778.

Waddell, Joseph Addison. *Annuals of Augusta County, Virginia from 1726 to 1871*. Augusta, VA: C.R. Caldwell, 1902.

Withers, Alexander S., Reuben Gold Thwaites and Lyman Copeland Draper. *Chronicles of Border Warfare, Or, A History of the Settlement by the Whites, of North-western Virginia, and of the Indian Wars and Massacres in that Section of the State*. Cincinnati, OH: Robert Clarke Company, 1895.

Wonning, Paul R. *A Year of Colonial American History: Little Known Obscure and Famous Historical Facts*. Indiana: Mossy Feet Books, 2015.

Young, Chester Raymond. *Westward into Kentucky: The Narrative of Daniel Trabue*. Lexington: University Press of Kentucky, 2015.

Zenzen, Joan M. *Fort Stanwix National Monument: Reconstructing the Past and Partnering for the Future*. Albany: State University of New York Press, 2008.

ABOUT THE AUTHOR

B obbi Dawn Rightmyer is a lifelong native of Harrodsburg, Kentucky, and she writes books of narrative historical nonfiction. Her books include *Harrodsburg* (Images of America series), *A History of Harrodsburg: Saratoga of the South* and *Born and Raised*. She also writes historical articles for the *Harrodsburg Herald*, *Kentucky Monthly*, the *Advocate-Messenger*, *Kentucky Humanities*, *Kentucky Explorer*, *Kentucky Living* and the *Lexington Herald-Leader*. She is also the administrator of the "Harrodsburg Sestercentennial" page on Facebook. Her website is HarrodsburgSestercentennial.com.